HARP UNSTRUNG

by

Ann M. Kucera

UNIVERSITY EDITIONS, Inc.
1905 Madison Avenue
Huntington, West Virginia 25704

This is a work of fiction. Any resemblance of any of the characters to persons living or dead is strictly coincidental.

FIRST EDITION

Copyright 1999, Ann M. Kucera
Library of Congress Catalog Card No: 98-90714
ISBN: 1-56002-853-X

Cover by Tristan Creeley

DEDICATION

FOR ALEX FRIEDMANN

MY INDEFATIGABLE COACH AND CHEER-LEADER.

HARP IN BOSTOWN

The sun rose cheerlessly over the National Cemetery. A time-lock released the catches on the doors of the pit-mouth and the licensed beggars crept slowly out of the tiny ornate stone structure which marked the descent into the Park Street Pit. They shook the night's ashes off themselves and shivered in the cold which penetrated their gray rags and raised goose pimples on their flesh. The pigeons that had spent the night on the quaint iron roof of the entrance, warming themselves in the hot rising air, flew away with much fuss. They knew no scraps would be forthcoming from the derelicts, most of whom shook from deprivation of both food and alcohol as well as from the cold.

Few of the beggars, known locally as Ghouls, ventured far from the opened doors, for some warmth still emanated from the dusty pit at the foot of the stone stairs. The tin cups handcuffed to their wrists would remain empty for two hours yet, until the tourist tube started shooting the first worshipers out onto the ground at eight sharp. Meanwhile there was nothing for the Ghouls to do except rummage through the nearest waste cans for half-eaten food scraps left behind in the late hours after the evening lock-up.

They also searched in the waste cans for bits of abandoned clothing to add to their rags, and kicked at the dry grass under the benches looking for dropped coins. One of them found a hat, and there was an angry scramble and a cry of pain as the prize was twisted out of his hands. Some of the shivering wretches drank water from the insulated stand pipe and others straggled away to relieve themselves in the Frog Pond, an open sewer nearby.

Harp McCuddy, a young man who shouldn't have been there at all because he was not licensed, shook himself indignantly free from ashes. His dark green coverall was filthy but not really in rags. His eyes were red, but he could see through them well enough, his lips were closed firmly and his thin body was still upright. He had been locked into the pit with the others, rounded up by the Horsemen who had not paused to check him for either a handcuffed cup or a badge, the ticket to the warm ashy bed. This morning his stomach was a little queasy but otherwise his faculties were in good condition. He told himself carefully that the queasiness must have been caused by hunger, not alcohol deprivation.

Harp was barely seventeen, the son of a moonshiner in one of the Nature Preserves. After his father's death he had quickly consumed the food in the larder and all of the whiskey. And on attempting to make more he had broken the delicate glass tubes of the still, not having listened properly to his father's instructions. Since the making and drinking of whiskey were all he really knew, the confused orphan had sold the family hovel to the first person who asked for it, and taking the handful of change offered had paid his fare to Bostown, where he had learned he could indulge his need for alcohol in the thin beer available to all alcoholics who could reach this Mecca.

After he had relieved himself at the Frog Pond Harp stretched and studied his surroundings. He had arrived here on the last tourist tube of the night before. This morning the appearance of the great national monument was new and thrilling to him. At one end of the rolling tree-filled cemetery stood the Lying-in-State House, its golden dome glistening in the morning sun. He knew from his school books that the gold leaves covering it had been brought from Ireland ages before by flocks of goldfinches that had pressed their tiny throbbing hearts and golden breast feathers against the dome before flying back forever across the wild dark sea. He gazed reverently up the hill at the noble building.

Behind it rose the white towers of the Terminal Hospital where the rich expired comfortably before their bodies were displayed in the State House and then borne to the underground crematorium. The poor and even middle-class dead were shot more conveniently into the crematorium from the tourist tubes during the late night hours when live travel was prohibited. Rich and poor alike served to heat the edifices of the cemetery: the State House, the Hospital, the Office Building and dormitories for the workers, the Palace and the stables for the horses and the Horsemen.

He had learned from a brochure he had picked up in the tourist tube that long ago the bodies of the city's dead had been bricked up in the innumerable niches of the pit walls, but space failing after the destruction of the rest of the city by the Great Tidal Wave, the crematoriums of the pit became the repository for the dead of the entire shrunken country, or at least for those dead whose bodies were not needed elsewhere for practical purposes. Individual land-wasting interment had become illegal since the rise to power of the Aubudon Society, and by its strict decrees all the dead became mingled dust, removed as needed through the hatches outside the sea wall, loaded onto great barges and returned to enrich the farms and forests.

The grassy park above ground was only a roof over the furnace below and a showplace to support the monuments of those groups and individuals important enough to be remembered. The cemetery was also the home for alcoholics, useless in the larger world, but here serving as a tourist attraction. The derelicts nightly enjoyed the free housing and the residual warmth of the cooling dead in the crematorium ash pit at the foot of the wide stairs.

Harp followed an active group of Ghouls which had begun to overturn some of the larger waste cans. Their findings were unappetizing but they continued to scrabble through the trash, ready to pounce, each one remaining a safe distance from his peevish neighbor. Harp did not look forward to defending any edibles he might find and walked briskly away under the frosty jewel-like trees. Several squirrels poured down the giant trunks;

some of them ran to his feet and sat up begging, paws crossed over their breasts. He felt sorry that he had nothing for them. Here and there in the brown grass stood a small stone marker. "Sacred to the memory of the Apache Indians who perished in the battle of the Carolina Mountains. 1563" read one. Another proclaimed "In honor of Nursing Supervisors, Everywhere"

On he went, irritably wanting a drink, warmth and food. When he chanced to look up he found that he had traveled almost the whole length of the cemetery without noticing the ponds, statues and little decorative buildings above the several entrances to the crematorium. Before him rose the high-walled Royal Palace which marked the end of the cemetery; beyond that he could see only the rusty fence and the blackened rubble leading down to the littered sea, the result of both flood and war. He shivered and mused on the ugliness before him. But he knew there was now universal peace, if not plenty. Here there was security, if not joy. Though paradise was limited to Nature Preserves and small parks like this one, both Mankind and the Universe were relatively safe, now that the Aubudon Society had taken charge.

He retraced his steps along the neat graveled paths of this skimpy paradise, hoping that enough time had elapsed for the worshipers to have emerged from the tubes, their pockets full of silver and tokens to put into the begging cups or scatter before the Ghouls, who could use them to buy beer from the beer wagons which were already starting to emerge from the bulkheads of the State House, their striped awnings fluttering gaily, ready for business the instant the first worshipers hit the ground.

From then on the day for the Ghouls would be continual sloshings of beer, with brief gobblings of packaged chips, while the worshipers doted and paid. At night would come the warm soft dusty drugged sleep in the pit. Or so he had heard was the life here, the only place on earth meant for a drunkard like him.

He heard the loud pop which signaled the disembarking of the first lot of worshipers, almost immediately followed by the inviting musical cry of "Beee-ah!" His steps lightened along with his heart, and he sped with the Ghouls toward the sound. Before he had sprinted more than half the distance he heard the thud of approaching hooves. He looked around wildly for a hiding place but the bushes were bare of leaves. He slipped off the path and crouched behind some twiggy shrubs, but the Horsemen quickly surrounded him, sitting high on their muscular steeds, which gleamed darkly as they stamped their feet and snorted threateningly through their flared nostrils. The Horsemen looked all-powerful in their silver ornamented uniforms and Harp, peeking up from his crouched position thought that he had never seen a more grand and frightening sight. His heart throbbed violently in his chest.

"Badge?" the nearest one shouted.

"I lost it," Harp mumbled. His captors laughed derisively and shook their whips at him.

"Out of here by the noon tourist vehicle or you'll go into the crematorium just as you are!" roared another.

"Yes, Sir," he sobbed.

"Ah, me boy," said their leader, a solid calm-looking man who peered down on him with pity in his eyes. "You look like you have the makings of a real boozer. Perhaps you'll be a Ghoul yet! Apply at the hospital; they'll issue you a badge if you're bona fide. You're welcome here if you are. It's the fakers we have to keep out! Go to the red door in the hospital basement." He pointed the way with his whip. "But a reminder.... If you don't have a badge by noon.... Well, wait and see." He chuckled unpleasantly and waved his fellows on as he wheeled his shining steed and cantered away. Harp's mouth hung open at the beauty of the sight. In all his life he could not remember having encountered such magnificence. His hope restored by the leader's helpful words, he headed toward the hubbub at the other end of the cemetery.

The worshipers were beginning to fan out from the mouths of the tourist tubes. Some began by kneeling in a bewildered manner before every marker. Others wandered aimlessly around, looking for a pretty enough place to leave their flowers. Most of the visitors were elderly though there were a few brightly dressed young adults and children. Some groups had leaders who marshaled and lectured;

the rest of them were already following the Ghouls, who were much more interesting than the monuments. They seemed to fascinate the orderly worshipers, who were neatly dressed in clean coveralls whose colors denoted their age, sex, and social position. The Ghouls, in contrast, were free spirits, untrammeled by social conformity, at one with Nature, admired too. The Ghouls had only to hold out their chained cups to be offered tokens which they could exchange for beer or potato chips. They smelled bad and their clothes were disgusting, but the visiting children were advised to admire them for their advanced spirituality.

The worshipers could buy wholesome refreshments at kiosks which sold sandwiches and non-alcoholic beverages. The Ghouls were allowed to mingle and ask their benefactors for left-over scraps and sometimes succeeded in prying food out of the hands of unwitting children, which they hurriedly chomped under the eyes of their envious peers. But had any worshipers desired to steal way to the beer wagons and load up on illegal beverages, the attendants, who were dressed quaintly in striped shirts, long aprons and black elastic arm garters, with black derbys on the backs of their pomaded heads, would drive them away with blows from their whips.

Encouraged by their breakfasts, the Ghouls began their daily performance. One wild-eyed filthy old fellow was leaping about haranguing the worshipers. He seemed angry and pointed from side to side and in front and in back of himself. He attracted a good-sized crowd. A group of female Ghouls had formed a dancing troupe and wiggled obscenely in a ragged chorus line. Some single performers told incomprehensible toothless jokes. A token fell to the ground beside Harp; he was on it in an instant, scrabbling it from the rough path, and breaking free from the milling crowd, he headed for the beer wagons. No one noticed that he had no badge; his bloodshot eyes and dirty clothes seemed proof enough that he belonged. He gulped his beer and crunched his potato chips.

He watched the performance of the Ghouls for a while to gather a few pointers, for he was determined to make a good job of his new career. Already the memory of his mountain home was growing dim, for Harp lived chiefly in the present. But he did recall he needed proof that he was an alcoholic in order to stay here, so he spoke to an idle Ghoul.

"Mister, will you tell me where to find the hospital with the red door?"

"That way, asshole," the Ghoul instructed helpfully. He followed a cement walk as directed and found himself standing at the end of a long line of nervous shivering men and women, which extended backward from the big red door all the way to the spot where the path intersected a gravel road that appeared to encircle the huge building.

Harp stood at this windy crossroad for a few minutes; the line was not moving at all. He spoke to the dirty bent woman standing in front of him.

"How much longer are we going to have to wait?" But she just shivered and laughed foolishly. He found he was shivering too, in spite of his breakfast of beer and chips, for he was not used to crowds, nor waiting at crossroads in the cold.

Giving up his original purpose in his lackadaisical way, he wandered down the emptier and more inviting route. It led him halfway around the building. There seemed to be no more doors and he was about to continue around the circle, which would no doubt lead him past the ornate marble motor entrance for the sick, the even more ornate exit for the dead, and so on until he returned to his unpromising starting point, when he noticed what might be a door behind a wedge of evergreens. There was no sidewalk leading to it, only a narrow path, a flattening of the brittle grass like the track of deer to a stream, but he parted the branches anyway out of curiosity.

It was a door, and a new one, for the cement around the frame was fresh and bits of mortar littered the pine needles beneath the trees. The door was made of smooth metal painted light gray, the color of the foundation next to it. It was not at all like the big red door which he should have entered, but it might be a quick way into the coveted building.

He squirmed deeper into the scratchy tree branches, well aware that he shouldn't be there. The door proved not only to be unlocked but a thin line of light around the edges showed that it was even a little ajar. He peered at the crack but could see nothing inside. A gentle push swung the door soundlessly open. He jumped back into cover, but there was no one there, neither inside the building nor behind him. The hospital windows high on the wall above stared down like sightless black eyes. He looked up and down the road before advancing.

The door opened onto a low-ceilinged hallway, clean and new and gray, in character rather like the tourist tube. The light was dim and the corridor disappeared around a corner about fifteen feet away. He crept softly along the spongy light gray floor, looking back from time to time to make sure his way of escape was open. There was no sound, not even that of breathing. Intensely aware of the unwisdom of his actions, for he was relatively sober, having drunk only one cup of beer that morning and no whiskey at all, but nevertheless lured on by his desire to penetrate the building and its mysteries and confident that he would emerge from this adventure with a shiny Ghoul's badge pinned to his chest, he crouched to a low crawling posture, like a cat creeping up on game, and peeked around the corner with his chin barely six inches above the floor.

The corridor came to an abrupt end in a brightly lit shining silver box which was almost as wide and as high as the corridor itself. Inside, seated on a tall metal stool, was a young woman dressed in a stiff white smock. She held a book in one hand and a tall glass in the other. Her attention was on the book. Harp first noticed that her legs were long and shapely. They began at the rung halfway up the stool and progressed to a pair of knees, slightly apart, then turned into two soft thighs which disappeared into a starched garment that was buttoned nearly to her neck. In the passing moment he noticed that her legs were perfectly clean, a sort of peach color on which grew almost imperceptible down of a lighter hue.

His eyes traveled next to her face, which was framed in long, slightly striped blond hair. It was a beautiful face, refined and spiritual; it bore a delicate look of noble suffering. She was clean all over, her garment was spotless and nothing dirty was caught in her hair. Even after he had left the tree-shaded hovel which he used to call home, and mingled with the busy traveling tourists, he had never seen a perfectly clean girl before.

He did not have time to tell the color of her lowered eyes for his glance traveled down to the tops of her breasts which showed a little under the stiff garment. He was so absorbed by the sight that it was fully three seconds before he became aware of a familiar appetizing aroma. Electrified, he located its source: the full glass that she held unnoticed in one hand while the other held the book she perused so diligently. It was unmistakably whiskey, crying out to him from a sea of beery looking bubbles. His desires having suddenly gotten out of control, he backed out of sight behind the corner on elbows and knees, straightened up swiftly, ran his fingers through his hair, glanced complacently at his deplorable coverall of nature-preserve green, and, advancing around the corner, approached the blond vision like a debonair chimney sweep. He had entered the silver box and was standing within a foot of the beautiful girl before she noticed him. She raised her head slowly and her pale blue eyes showed no surprise as they swept upwards from his feet. She held the tantalizing glass out to him.

"Here, drink this," she remarked in an easy conversational tone. He seized the glass in both hands without waiting to say thank-you; after all, he had not had anything to drink except one small cup of beer since the previous morning. He gulped half of it at once, not really minding the watery bubbles that assailed the inside of his nose. When he slowed down to savor the rest, and to appreciate the wonder of her company, he found that a door had slid shut behind him, the floor was rumbling and an uncertain feeling had attacked his legs. He looked at the blank walls and at the girl, but she was already deep in her book again.

He decided to compromise between panic at being imprisoned in an escape-proof box, and reluctance to reveal his unease to the girl, by drinking the rest of the whiskey. The elevator, for that is what it was, rose very slowly. He finished the glass and by shuffling and coughing attracted her attention.

"Did you enjoy your drink?" she murmured in a pleasantly attentive voice.

"I needed that," he said feelingly, relief and friendship

flooding over him. He became garrulous under her interested eye. "My first real drink in two days!" She quietly made a mark on a slip of paper lying in her book, using a sharp pencil she had retrieved from the cleft in her bosom. She smiled vaguely.

"Yes?" she prompted. So very slow was the elevator, and so pleased was he to see that someone was expending handwriting on his behalf, that by the time he rehearsed his major symptoms, which were clamoring in his mind for attention in competition with the desire to touch her, the door on the opposite side of the elevator had opened to announce that they had arrived. By that time he was beginning to feel the effect of the whiskey, so he emerged with her into the large busy windowless room with confidence and a cheerful smile.

The near end of the room was occupied by several desks at which sat white-coated women busily writing things in folders, or else inspecting little square machines like the ones he had seen at the counter where he had bought his ticket for the tourist tube. The women got up from time to time and passed through doors lining the walls. They were all very ordinary women, though clean, and none of them had beauty in the least like that of the girl in the elevator.

At the other end of the room were a number of red plastic armchairs alternating with black plastic tables. Most of the chairs were occupied by ragged dirty men who were holding glasses and chatting amiably among themselves. On the tops of the black tables stood a quantity of emptied glasses and some that were quite full. One of the Horsemen stood idly behind them. Quite forgetting the girl, who had melted into the background, he went confidently forward, knowing his place now. He found a chair for himself, exchanged his empty glass for a full one from a nearby table and started to relate his recent adventures to his new friends. He wondered why the Horseman did not pull up a chair and take a load off his feet.

The whole group was mellow, and became more so. The irritability of the early risers was completely absent. They received new recruits from the elevator about every thirty minutes. Harp observed their arrival out of a comfortable haze, and noticed that when the beautiful girl in the short coat went into the elevator alone she would emerge a half-hour later with a bemused man like himself following her. Some were badly dressed, like Harp; some were scarcely covered with rags. All were nearly sober when they stepped out of the elevator.

Sandwiches were served by one of the white-coated women at noon exactly. Harp, who could tell time and read fairly well, noted this from a huge clock on the wall which not only told the hours, but also the days of the week. It was decorated with many intriguing little clock-faces set into it.

Every so often another woman passed through the relaxed group of drinkers and pressed spoon-sized sticks for a short time into their grumbling mouths, and wrapped straps much too tightly around their upper arms. But since the men got a good look down the top of her coat as she leaned over them, their grumbling was half-hearted. She also made a mark on each man's right ear lobe with a small rubber stamp. From time to time another one of the women would lead a sleepy subject by the hand and disappear with him through one of the doors.

Harp had maintained a sorry sort of vigilance throughout the morning's adventures; now he relaxed under the cheerful attendance of the white-coated women. The appearance of lunch on plates and a constant supply of filled glasses completed his feeling of ease. Certain that he was in kind medical hands, indeed the only officially kind hands that a mountain hovel-dweller was ever likely to know, and sure that he would soon acquire a Ghoul's license, he leaned back in foggy security and let the whiskey put him to sleep.

He stirred briefly at the regular medical ministrations, but when he awoke fully, in need of a bracing drink, the clock told him that it was ten past five. He drank a half glass, got up and relieved himself in a tiny washroom, having watched the others make urgent dashes to the same door. There were fewer men seated around him now, all asleep, sprawling and snoring except for two who were growling nastily at each other. The women at the desks had left; only the Horseman remained, standing wakefully behind the chairs. Harp twisted around and looked at him; he didn't seem to have quite the same face he had had before. Harp took another sip to make sure. He began to think about supper.

There was a knock on one of the doors and the Horseman unlocked and opened it. Two more Horsemen strode in, walked expressionlessly to the nearest of the two arguing men and led him firmly between them out the door.

More time passed. The Horsemen returned and bore the other man away. Harp was really getting hungry and tried to solace himself with more sips. The Horsemen appeared again and came toward him.

"Where are we going?" he asked suspiciously, squirming to avoid their touch on his arms. One of them clamped a large hand just above his elbow; it was his old acquaintance from that morning, the one who had made the joke about putting him in the crematorium. He suddenly realized that it was long past noon and he still had not obtained a badge. Was it possible that the Horseman had really meant what he had said about burning him alive? That it wasn't just a joke?

Harp felt that he was going to throw up, but first he would fight. He began to scream, half in hope of frightening his attackers and half in mindless terror. He braced his arms and legs against the door frame but he was no match for the Horsemen as they dragged him through.

BEWARE OF DR. FISH

When the crowds of worshipers had seen everything there was to be seen and had become thoroughly bored, they returned the way they had come, buying their inexpensive tickets at the entrance to the tourist tube, hanging about with people of their own sort (easily recognized by their coveralls) grumbling about the service, commenting wittily about the Ghouls, craning their necks for a glimpse of the Horsemen and dropping their refuse tidily into the trash receptacles. Those who were extremely patriotic waited until the noon gong and then scurried across the cemetery to the Palace in order to attend the royal audience at exactly half past twelve.

There was no question of actually touching the hand of the young prince or one of the three princesses; there were far too many worshipers for that. Nor could they get into the palace or obtain any other glimpse of them, for it was well known that the young royals never stirred from the building, and all the windows were opaque. But they would see one of them perform the daily ceremony of the Bath from behind the high steel mesh fence which surrounded the Great Pool.

The Great Pool was the only one of its kind still in existence. There were archaeological remains here and there, but so high was the price of water that none had ever been restored. Indeed there was no reason to do so, since hardly anyone knew how to swim any more except those fortunate enough to live near a lake (now mostly fenced in as reservoirs) or an accidental pool in a stream. Anyone who braved the ocean water was likely to come down with parasites or deadly diseases.

The high fence was soon lined with worshipers, their noses pressed devoutly into the gaps of the mesh. They had a clear view of the gaunt gray Palace. The pool with its scattering of little trees in tubs on the narrow surround looked like a wide blue carpet leading up to the small ornate door at one corner of the building. A well-muscled healthy young man emerged, wearing a large white towel like a toga. His features were regular, handsome and bland; his hair was blond and curled all over his head. He raised one hand to the level of his face and moved it from side to side as though he were half waving and half sketching a blessing. But he did not look at the crowd; his eyes were on the ground, his movements slow. He advanced to the rim of the pool and let the towel fall to his feet. He was entirely naked underneath and a great approving sigh rose from the assembled worshipers.

He stood without expression for the requisite five minutes, staring down at the water, and then stiffened his body, did a businesslike dive, swam briskly the length of the pool, turned and swam briskly back. As soon as he climbed the ladder and reached the place where he had left the towel he snatched it up and wrapping himself tightly, ran to the door, which someone from within held open for him.

That someone was Dr. Dapper, the prince's personal psychiatrist, who always attended the audiences at the pool. "Come into my office, Your Highness," he purred. "It's hot cocoa today!" The shivering young man rammed his feet into the slippers which awaited him just inside the doorway and bolted across the marble floor into a nearby room, at the same time yelling unmannerly insults at the psychiatrist, the assembled worshipers at the pool side, his family, his fate and anything else he could shout at, including the slippers which perversely tried to escape his feet.

Hence the psychiatrist. The three princesses had their own, a lady doctor whom they shared, being merely girls. The problem was the coldness of the water: The Aubudon Society would not allow it to be heated much above freezing lest some of the precious fluid evaporate and be wasted. There was no pool cover and the winter swims among the ice floes were torture; a general depression settled over the four royal siblings around the middle of September and lasted until the middle of June.

Of course all of them were also offended at having to parade naked in public, especially Anastasia who tended to put on fat. Robert the Bruce, known to his sisters as Brute, was the worst protester. He had threatened suicide several times, and once had been caught trying to insinuate himself, disguised, into the tourist tube. All three girls were now over fourteen so they could take turns with him at the performance of the Bath. It felt that their shouldering of part of the burden would help him develop a more manageable disposition, but that was not the case; prolonged exposure to the cold water only made the princesses irritable too. The fact that this appearance was their royal duty did not mitigate their suffering.

The necessity of keeping the cranky quartet happy was the constant preoccupation of the mentors. For in addition to placating the public, the duty of providing for the succession fell upon them, for there were no other royals. Any suitable young members of the Aubudon establishment brought in for their inspection either had their faces scratched by the girls or were booted by Brute, who unfortunately had been given Karate lessons when very young. The general atmosphere in the Palace was gloomy, and an endless stream of tutors and suitors traveled in one door and out the other.

"I realize, Prince," said Dr. Dapper disapprovingly, "that your life is not very rewarding, that the burden of self-sacrifice laid upon you for the good of mankind is tiresome." Brute, who was pressed up against the heat register, slurped his cocoa in an offensive way. Dr. Dapper was not perturbed; he assumed the stance of a lecturer. "But we must remember the lessons of ecological history, which show that any society lacking a focus with which all members can identify, eventually flies apart into the Evil Arms of Entropy. Long before your day mankind had a god, or gods; now that the notion of god has been relegated to the status of psychological aberration, there is no one left but you children to hold human society together in its proper niche. I'm sorry, but that's how it is. Reality must be faced."

Brute finished his cocoa in silence and then asked sarcastically if he might have permission to go to his room and put on his clothes. As usual, Dr. Dapper's lecture had fallen on deaf ears, and the psychiatrist turned his head away to show his displeasure. He did not see the prince stand up and sling his wet towel around his head, but he did feel the full force of the blow which almost knocked him off his chair, and he could hear through the enveloping stinging wetness the prince's loud angry laughter and the slamming of the office door behind him.

Dr. Dapper felt exhausted. He lay down on his couch to worry; he could not endure much more of this. But the Palace was a very comfortable place to live. He and his wife, who, under her maiden name, was the princesses' psychiatrist, would hate to have to leave and go huddle up in one of the beehive pod buildings at the other end of the tourist tube where the middle class lived. He squirmed at the thought, imagining the sensation of trying in vain to stretch his legs in one of the narrow shelf beds with which the pods were furnished.

If the boy could only be removed, the much younger and more malleable princesses might carry on the necessary traditions without alarming the populace, at least for a while. He dreamed briefly of murdering his patient and then pulled himself together. Brute might calm down and be easier to handle if he were allowed a sexual outlet. If girls refused to come to the palace, perhaps he could be let out to find his own mate: some girl who was not a member of the Aubudon Society and thus an object of hatred to the royal children, who blamed the Society for all their misfortunes, including the deaths of their parents from Pneumonia.

After becoming a father the prince might actually develop a sense of responsibility to his family, and remembering that they were hostages dependent on his good behavior, develop a more socially respondent attitude.

But the prince could not mingle with the general populace; he was too easily recognized and Dr. Dapper shuddered to think of the risk of infection. The unhappy psychiatrist was frustrated in all his attempts to find a solution. If only he could get the unreasonable boy off his hands, turn him over to some stronger authority which could control him. But who could control the head of a State? Only the head of a larger State.

That was it! He sat up abruptly. If the prince were made to visit the Imbalancia, the center of Empire, for a limited time only, as a Delegate, that powerful government might intimidate him into good behavior (he ground his teeth at the thought of it), or the miracle might occur that he would take the official belief in Universal Order to heart and turn his youthful energy to some productive purpose. The populace could do without their pretty prince for a short time. And he, Dr. Dapper, could temporarily assist his wife by providing a father-figure for the girls, especially Anastasia. He sighed at the thought of such a pleasant vacation.

He rolled off the couch and grabbed his communication translator. After only a few annoying hours he was in contact with the Masters of the Universe and had offered the high squeaking voice at the other end his solution to this dangerous and growing crisis on earth. To his chagrin he learned that they were quite aware of the situation (of course there were spies in the Palace; there have always been spies in palaces) and had already arrived at the same solution. He was ordered to implement it immediately.

Thus it was that Brute, hurriedly and haphazardly dressed, found himself ushered ingratiatingly into the department of Stellar Transportation Preparation (STP) on an upper floor of the great Hospital.

"If your highness would wait in here for just a moment," gushed the white coated lady attendant who coaxed him into a side room and urged him to sit in a red plastic arm chair. Dr. Dapper, who had dragged him away from his TV, not even allowing him time for supper or for saying good-bye to his sisters, was not permitted to go in with him. The attendant slid out of the door while Brute was looking at the other occupant of the room, who was seated in a straight-backed chair opposite to his.

He had never before seen such a miserable creature. Not

only was he thin and dirty, but his head hung down almost as though his neck were broken. He was fastened to the chair by several sets of handcuffs in an amateurish way with one arm down and one arm up. A long broad belt was wound around his chest and arms, securing him upright; the belt buckle, which was very large, had a portrait of a prancing horse stamped onto it.

But Brute did not notice these details at first. His immediate thought was, "Here is someone who is even more unhappy than I am." His heart went out to him. He wondered if the strange boy were being punished for trying to commit suicide, for Brute well remembered that only a few years before he had been strapped up and even stuffed into a bag after an attempt to hang himself—or perhaps that had been an exaggeration, for he had only insisted on wearing a noose for a necktie while his sisters jeered.

"What's your name?" he asked sympathetically.

"Harp McCuddy," was the dismal reply. "I only wanted to get a Ghoul's license and become a good citizen. Look what they did to me!"

"I'm Robert the Bruce. You may call me Prince. Would you like me to get those handcuffs off you?" He was already undoing the belt as he spoke. He was about to search out the white-coated woman and have her release the captive, for he had not yet learned that Dr. Dapper was not the only one who dared disobey his orders, but he spied a key on a table and snatching it up he released Harp, who collapsed onto the floor and started to cry.

Brute decided that he was a poor spineless thing and that he probably would not be suitable as a friend. But before the prince could turn his back and sit down, Harp crawled across the floor to him, wrapped his arms around one of his legs, laid his tearful grubby head against his knee and swore upon his mother's grave that he would be grateful to him as long as he lived.

"You can call on me for anything you ever want! I'll lay down my life for you. You've saved me and I know you'll go right on saving me because I'm your faithful slave and you're my faithful master. Everyone knows that I always keep my word. My word is sacred! The loyalty between us will never be broken! You don't happen to have a drink on you, do you?"

Brute was more than a little embarrassed and struggled in Harp's loyal grasp. "I don't have anything to drink just now. But sure, I'll look after you. I won't let anyone hurt you." He worked himself loose, playfully flexing a muscle to show Harp that he was strong enough to protect them both.

The inner door opened and the ravishing beauty who had lured Harp into the elevator slipped in, carrying a clip-board instead of a book. If she was surprised to see Harp unfastened from the chair she didn't show it. She still wore the same vague distant expression.

"Dr. Eustacia Fish," she murmured. "Your Highness, I presume." She did not look at Harp. "There are a few questions we need to have you answer in order to clear you for your departure. Also a short physical exam will be necessary. Your records are quite complete but they need updating. If you will both come with me?"

She drifted out the door and they followed, Brute first, eager, and Harp close behind, matching his pace to his protector's and almost stepping on his heels. Brute found this disagreeable and said so, but Harp was afraid to be left behind. They went down a corridor, down an elevator, down another corridor to a rather dreary part of the hospital, all zig-zag halls and little doors with frosted glass set into the upper halves. "This way, Mr. McCuddy." She had opened a door and was looking directly at Harp with glinting eyes. Without having time to think he walked in and it was shut immediately behind him.

He was in a large brightly lit room where everything was made of glass or metal. A number of white-clad people, both men and women, were sitting on stools or scurrying around with either rapt or indignant expressions. Some small motors were hugging and chugging. Several of the inhabitants converged on him briskly; they seemed to be in a terrible hurry.

"The Doctor will see you soon," barked a stiff knobby

lady. "There are just a few formalities to go through first." His garments were stripped from his body by hands so inoffensive and speedy that he could not find any one moment in which to protest. He was clucked at and encouraged to sit in a chair and be stuck with a needle to draw a large container of his blood. He was made to drink some disgusting liquid then urged to swallow a small camera and disgorge it again, was subjected to an enema and another camera, was endlessly photographed from head to foot, and lost a large patch of skin to a scalpel. The last part of the ordeal was very painful but they would not give up despite his beginning to whimper and plead. It finally took three men to hold him down during the removal of the large piece of his epidermis.

All of this activity was unfamiliar to him; he couldn't guess its purpose, as the inhabitants of the nature preserves were usually left alone by the medical profession to live or die in a natural way. Nearly all they saw of civilization were a few grades of school in a cold barn and visitations from noisy politicians in the same building. The tax collector however was readily available, and a dole of food was issued in the form of stamps to discourage the natives from killing the deer. So one must excuse him for his panic in such unfamiliar circumstances.

He next was stuffed into a very tight box which burst into loud booming noises, and when he tried to wiggle out he found he could not. He tried to drown out the booming with his screams but was unsuccessful. He had read a story about an ancient Indian who, when dying, sang his death song to give him courage, but that didn't work either. After it was all over they handed him a small towel to cover his nakedness, and when they opened a door for him he bolted through it.

He found himself in a small room with a bench along one wall. He sat there for hours, or so it seemed; there was no window so he could not tell how much time had passed. First he brooded over his injuries. After the soreness had subsided he examined the walls, floor and ceiling, all of which were bare of any irregularity except for a recessed light above him. There were three matching doors; he could not remember which one he had come through.

The bench was hard and it looked and smelled like someone had lost control of his bowels at one end of it.

Suddenly another man, clutching his towel to his naked body, plunged through a door which Harp now recognized by the gleam of the shining cutlery in the room behind it. Both he and the stooped newcomer were eager to share their recent experiences and demand sympathy from each other, but each was so wrapped up in his pains that he hardly noticed the other's. Harp finally recognized him as a fellow alcoholic and one of the beautiful doctor's fellow dupes. They both agreed that they wouldn't screw her if she begged them and that they were in serious need of a drink.

There soon came the noise of a key at one of the other doors and it opened to reveal two Horsemen waiting at the entrance to a dark corridor. Harp shrank up as small as he could, but they had not come for him. The led away the newcomer so quickly that he practically ran through the door with them. Harp thought, "I'm next," which caused his alcohol-deprived stomach to jump around and his hands to flutter also. The room was beginning to assume a disagreeable brightness. His bladder was nearly bursting, so he emptied it on the floor behind the bench for lack of any other place and felt a little better.

The first door opened again after a long wait and another towel-clad man staggered in, only to be removed almost immediately by the returning Horsemen. More hours seemed to crawl by.... He had to relieve himself again. Two more alcoholics staggered through and disappeared down the dark corridor with the Horsemen. Time passed and Harp began to hope that he had been overlooked. He paced and paced, avoiding the dirty corner. Walking seemed to do him good, for it occurred to him that they had possibly forgotten him, and that now was a good time to break out.

He tried the door he had come through; it was locked. Perhaps the Horsemen had forgotten to turn the key on their door. But it was firmly shut, too. He gave it a cranky retaliatory kick, bruised his bare toes and limped over to try the remaining door.

It was locked and he gave it a kick with the other foot. Then he knocked on it because it was after all a door.

To his surprise the lock snapped and the door swung open as though someone had been waiting on the other side for him to knock. He stood semi-naked on the threshold, looking into the serene eyes of the beautiful girl from the elevator. She had just seated herself behind a cluttered desk facing the door; there was a chair close beside her and she scraped some papers off it onto the floor.

"Won't you come in?" she asked pleasantly, indicating the empty chair. Without taking his eyes off her he entered and sat down, gingerly arranging the towel as he sat. The rug on the floor was very soft under his sore cold toes.

She arranged some papers on the desk in front of her. "Your tests show you to be nearly ideal for my purpose," she remarked, pulling her short coat down to better cover her legs.

He wondered what her purpose was. In this new life of his anything could happen. But she quickly answered his unspoken question, as though she had known what was in his mind and it had made her stern. "I am recruiting alcoholics for a medical experiment. I am sure you will be happy to know that despite your alcoholism you are in perfect health, except for a little unavoidable brain damage. I think you may come to actually enjoy the experiment." She pointed to a full glass on her desk behind a stack of papers, and Harp seized it gratefully.

"It is a commonly believed that alcoholism is an addiction. I prefer to think of it as incomplete adaptation. It is my intent to test the ability of the Human to adapt in his person and also in his genetic material to an Ethanol Ambience, gradually increasing in intensity. Yours will be the first generation. You will be trained to limit your dietary input almost entirely to alcohol, and may even be taught to breathe it a little. Breeding, of course, will be highly selective and future generations will perhaps be able to live on, breathe and swim in pure Ethanol, at which point they will form a colony on some temperate alcohol-based planet where they will survive fairly well without the need for water. Females will be selected after the initial difficulties have been cleared by male experimentation. Non-humans and botanicals as well as bacterial and viral entities will also take part in the process; however, frankly, I doubt if they will adapt. Only humans have so far exhibited tangible affinity for large quantities of Ethanol. It is for that reason that we have excluded alcohols other than Ethanol even though they too are abundant in available habitats. Your affinity in that direction is outstanding, your metabolism is excellent, your utilization is remarkable."

"Thank you," said Harp shyly.

"Only three of the men interviewed today came through the battery of tests with high enough grades to make them worth the outlay, which is enormous, I can assure you. This is also the last day that these hospital facilities will be available for male selection. You may ask questions if you wish; then you will have five minutes in which to make up your mind if you will participate or not."

"What's the pay?" he asked eagerly.

"I believe you have misunderstood me. There is no pay, for you will encounter nothing in the place to which you are going which can be purchased with money. You will be transported to the Imbalancia, where you will commence your new life-long experience, and then later to another climate when you are ready for it."

"Will you be there too?" he asked warily.

"I and other scientists will be beside you always. Our faces of course will change as the years go on. By the time your great grand children are born and grown up, hopefully on an Ethanol world, we will all have passed away. As for the present, you surely do not expect me to devote my talents to only one experiment, do you?" She slapped peevishly at her papers. "I have half a dozen in hand and more in the planning stages. But I can guarantee my presence part of the time, and the best of care all of the time. After all, this project is under the supervision of RES, a sub-branch of the Aubudon Society, and as you well know, their interest is your interest." She stood up as she named the august group. Harp stood up too and his towel fell off. He bent, flushing, to retrieve it, but she had not noticed.

"You have also received a high score in our survival tests. Your curiosity, though not outstanding, is adequate. You demonstrated your unwillingness to remain in an unpleasant dilemma when you entered the back door of the hospital, and later when you kicked and knocked on the door to my office. I don't mind telling you that I was worried. I waited for you to take action for more than an hour. Your time was nearly up, and in light of the shortage of male subjects that would have been very unfortunate. Now, if you have no further questions, you must make up your mind. Five minutes if you please." She looked at a small clock chained to her wrist.

Harp bent his torso forward in what he hoped was a posture of contemplative thought. Actually there was no doubt in his mind about what he wanted to do, but he needed to conceal his joy at the prospect of his new life encased in a womb of his favorite sustaining fluid to make it appear that he was the one conferring the favor, not she.

"I've got to have time off. I can't work every day," he stipulated.

"There will be no work, of course. All your time will be your own," agreed the lovely Dr. Fish. "With the exception of a few hours for tests of your progress. Urine tests, mainly," she reassured him, seeing him draw back into his chair a little. "There will be attendants to see to your every need." She began to warm to the subject, extending her arms. "Luxurious surroundings, free Terror video, every elegance that can be accommodated to the Ethanol environment without spoilage. As you become acclimated, perhaps you can be issued your own adapted Fastar. Your contribution to science will not go unrewarded, you may be sure!"

"How about the other guys? What are you going to give them?" he asked jealously.

"I was just going to mention them when your question arose," she said virtuously, with her eyes riveted on one point in the cornice of the room. "As you can imagine, not all the subjects tested and interviewed showed quite your physical stamina or strength of character as evinced by your abundant curiosity. Several showed liver, spleen, heart, brain or other physical damage. A few, though in good physical condition, were too chronologically challenged to make it practical to embark on a long-term project. Some could not show long enough histories of alcohol intake or else showed poor alcohol adaptation. There were only three perfect young males who burned alcohol like their mother's milk, so to speak. Two were curiously enough of Irish extraction and one was French.

"What are their name?" he asked.

"Their names will not be of interest to you. As it turns out, all the other applicants except yourself had to be rejected. I am even of two minds whether it will be worth my while to proceed with you alone, such a small sample, such a waste of manpower! If you do not cooperate fully I may have to re-program my collecting techniques and begin again. All wasted!" She sighed plaintively. "No, I take that back; there was one man, just one who was far enough gone to be licensable as a Ghoul. He was given his permit and sent on his way, with, I may say, the blessing of the entire hospital staff. He was very grateful. The others have rejoined their families."

"You kicked the two O.K. ones out too?" he inquired reproachfully.

"They were not willing to cooperate," she said, fingering a small pink swelling under her chin which he had not noticed before.

"Hey, maybe I could think it over some more," he stammered.

"Your time for questioning is up," she advised him. "But before you say yes or no I must tell you that the two suitable but unwilling subjects also rejoined their families."

"What are you getting at?" he asked dubiously.

"If they had been ordinary people without alcoholic tendencies our regulations would have made us return them to society via the tourist tube; we might even have paid the fares for the indigent ones. However, alcohol consumption is illegal everywhere except here in the cemetery, and if we were to aid and abet them to continue drinking in the larger world we would become accessories before the fact. With the exception of the successful Ghoul, the rest were assigned rooms in the hospital."

Harp stopped breathing for a moment.

Yes," she said. "Our budget did not allow them to enjoy a full scale lying-in-state ceremony under the golden dome, but you will be happy to hear that they had a mass group display on the porch, lasting a full twenty minutes, before going on to the crematorium."

For a time Harp pictured himself among them, but the thought quickly melted in his habitual optimism and faith in his good luck, or whatever it was that made him open doors. His alcoholic future loomed a bit less deliciously, that was all. So he was to be some kind of prisoner, allowed to live on good behavior. Well he would show them! As soon as he had fully slaked his thirst, some weeks from now, he would exercise his wits and give them the slip. They would have spent a small fortune on him, and for nothing! It would be a good joke.

"I can see from your face that you have decided to accept our offer," she remarked, and extending a graceful arm and finger, touched a buzzer wired to her desk.

"One of our attendants will see you to your temporary quarters before transit. I suggest a bath with plenty of soap; fresh clothing will be provided. There will be a nurse ready to give you your first alcohol rub as soon as you are clean. Then a glass of whiskey for supper with a supplementary IV of glucose on demand, though I imagine you will not feel much sugar deprivation until some time tomorrow. We take ship for the Imbalancia at nine in the morning, sharp." She began to study her papers, and did not see his face as he turned to gawk at the incoming Horsemen.

THE IMBALANCIA

Early the next morning, after a liquid breakfast with a square of agar for substance, the nurse led Harp down a corridor into a small room equipped with a video screen. Two reclining chairs stood at one end and in one of them lay Brute, busily finishing off a large breakfast on a tray. They greeted each other enthusiastically, like shipwrecked mariners. Harp lay down in his chair and was strapped in by the nurse, who cheerily informed him that it was for his own good to prevent his indulging in solid food and spoiling his health. She attempted to take away Brute's unfinished tray but he vehemently objected and she backed off.

The nurse, Miss Squieze, was not a disagreeable young woman; she was only obeying orders. She was quite plump and had tightly curled red hair and freckles, and bounced a little under her white coat when she moved. She turned on the video machine facing the chairs, moved to the door, switched off the light and left the room.

When he was sure she had gone, Harp stretched out his hand as far as it would go toward Brute's nearly empty plate. He need not have bothered for Brute was on his feet and handing him the tray before he could even ask for it. Harp ate his second, more substantial breakfast in the half light given off by the screen, which showed a rotund gentlemen dressed in a black academic coverall and wearing the flat-topped hat of his profession, speaking to a group of dozing students. The lecture was already well underway.

"...the Imbalancia, the giant space ship containing the General Assembly of the Aubudon Society, is in constant motion as it cruises from Galaxy to Galaxy, from individual star system to individual star system, from planet to planet, from moon to asteroid, not missing a single area where life can possibly exist, be found, and be guarded from extinction. And at each of these far flung locations it stops for a short while to inspect the ecological condition of the inhabitants, to make the necessary robotic repairs and improvements to its space-bombarded surface, and to take on and disembark passengers. This much every child knows."

At this point Harp was already asleep, helped off to dreamland by his morning Ethanol, agar and a good breakfast besides. The voice of the droning professor did not keep him awake for he lectured in Esperanto, which was unknown to Harp. Brute, of course was fluent in the language but had heard this particular speech many times before, so he too dropped off to sleep. Part of this lecture by Dr. V. Nox, a Fellow of the I.S.P.E. at Cushion University, is reproduced here, translated into Bostonian for the benefit of the gentle reader. Only part, however, for general interest in his subject matter is slight. Dr. Nox is probably the only human alive who thoroughly understands the mechanics of the Aubudon society; most of mankind merely accepts them gratefully.

To continue: "As thinking adults, however, we may delve deeper into the question. Every civilization so far discovered in the universe is represented in the Aubudon Society, and furthermore, each civilization has its own name for that distinguished assemblage. Indeed, simple logic will demonstrate that it is impossible for its ancient original name to have been "Audubon Society" as some earthbound diehards assert, for its existence is known to predate that of Earth itself, even to predate the formation of our life-giving sun. And since research has shown that the word "Audubon" derives from French and its antecedent Latin, and means loosely "sounds good", which refers to the song of birds, and since French and Latin are not nor have provably been spoken elsewhere than on Earth, it follows as night the day, and day the night, that the name "Audubon Society" occurred after the creation of the earth with its multiple tongues, and hence postdates the founding of the society itself. There are some scoffers who believe that the Imbalancia herself does not predate the Earth, but that is patently ridiculous.

"The Imbalancia is an old vessel and partly unserviceable. This is due entirely to a failure to establish fiscal responsibility for the ship's upkeep at the inception of the organization. As an unhappy result the maintenance of each unit, each insulated habitat, each cell, is under the control of, and furnished at the expense of, the delegate or his world. I say unhappily. Why? Because during the life-time of the Aubudon Society, which stretches so far back into the history of the universe that the young people of today would have difficulty imagining it without the aid of a computer, numerous worlds represented at the assembly have experienced super-novas and other final catastrophes, leaving their delegate or delegates stranded at the assembly. They thus become the only surviving members of their species, isolated forever in their protective cubicles at the expense of the society, carefully preserved by subscription, to ride forever safe, encapsulated through the starry deeps. And some of them have remarkable longevity.

"How many of these intelligent endangered life forms exist is not exactly known, communication problems being what they necessarily are aboard the Imbalancia. Though there is some pre-arranged form of communication with the home planet, in such a diverse group there can be little communication, no general assembly place, no leaving of one's cubicle with its carefully controlled atmosphere. Instead all conversation is carried on by phone, speaking tubes, electronic tappers and sometimes by beating on drums and banging on the walls. It is frequently necessary to relay conversations through neighbors' facilities, as each cubicle is attached to the main body of the ship at the point where it first hit its target. Cubicles are fastened to cubicles, often completely covered by them; indeed, no human has been able, as far as I know, to ascertain the original appearance of the

Imbalancia beneath its motley exterior, and certainly no one from Earth has ever been permitted to enter the main body of the ship, which is believed by those who lovingly trace its progress through the heavens by radio waves to travel by the old method of gravo-drive, slow but reliable.

"The cubicles, or homes of the delegates, are designed by the worlds they represent and are attached by the robots who swarm over the body of the ship as it rests temporarily on solid ground; in dry-dock as it were. (chuckle! chuckle!) Earth's cell contains beautiful hydroponic gardens for use during periods of difficult navigation when the Imbalancia is not readily accessible to the supply shuttles which make regular visits.

"Earth's corps of delegates lives in a carefully designed ellipsoid maintained at a comfortable warmth. You will remember that our cell is a fortunate latecomer; therefore there is an unobstructed view for its inhabitants via a specially built porthole, through which they may observe the sky, the stars, the Universe.

"Our delegates receive regular instruction by taco-grav as well as regular visits from supply ships which bring them reinforcements and comforts from Earth whenever we are in proper juxtaposition to make such contact possible. During the present decade, due to astral positioning, taco-grav messages cannot be sent or received. It has been almost six years since the last shuttle got through; our best calculations are that there will be a short window of opportunity for another shuttle in about twenty-eight months.

"But our brave delegates continue to carry on their meaningful task, that of assisting the Aubudon Society in its thorough inspection of the Universe. They have a single, but I am sure, significant voice in the assembly's decisions which so affect our lives, nay our very existence. Our delegates have been provided with the loudest electronic communicators permitted by the rules of the assembly, so we may be sure our voice is heard. Therefor we confidently put into practice the Society's decisions and obey the orders which have been relayed to us here on Earth, knowing that they have issued from the combined intelligences of the Society, including those of our carefully selected delegates, young people painstakingly educated for their mission, drawn from our brightest most promising youth, both male and female.

"Someday, not in our generation, nor indeed during the calculated lifetime of our species, but someday, far in the future, The Aubudon Society will have finished its tour of inspection and come once more to Earth on its second or third time around, as it did (and just in time) during the sixth narrow avoidance of World War III. They will find on their arrival that we and our descendants have kept the faith. Even now recycling and population growth are under control; Man will shortly reach his full potential, graciously filling his niche, no more and no less. During the lifetime of nearly everyone I see before me in this lecture hall, the Orthopteran Blattidae, presently invading our human space, will be confined to warm tropical isles where they may breed and raise their cockroach young in peace, safe from hostile predatory attack...."

Inside their carefully designed comfortable elliptical cell the three delegates from Earth were going through their daily routines. Dr. Irma Scriema, the physicist and ranking delegate, was doing the dishes after the evening meal. Although the light shone blindingly through the dingy glass of the single round port hole, the wall chronometer read 19 hours earthtime and Al and Wiener insisted on eating supper at 6 PM sharp. Dr. Irma wore a faded, amorphous house dress put together from scraps of coveralls, but it was shapely enough to reveal the outline of her gravid belly on which she repeatedly wiped her soapy hands, leaving a large damp spot. Her hair was stringy, her nails bitten to the quick, her expression furtive and hostile. A baby cried shrilly and incessantly from an adjoining cubicle.

Dr. Al Kapital, the political economist, was slouched in a home-made armchair, leaning back against a frayed pillow and smoking a rag-like substance in a short length of copper tubing. His once-white buttonless jacket was stuffed into a filthy pair of trousers with holes at the knees; a curly black beard nearly obscured his face and was distinguished from the hair on his chest only by its superior greasiness. Dr. Wiener von Brane was hunkered down in a corner, his back against a bulkhead, cleaning his nails with a kind of scalpel. His hair was stringy but combed, and his long thin nervous face was nicked by the attacks of dull razors. His clothes were also filthy but patched at the knees. He was Irma's botanic assistant and had been the navigator of the cell on its flight from Earth.

A power-play only a few months after their arrival at the Imbalancia had established Irma as the cook, the bedfellow of the two men and the one responsible for weeding the hydroponics, which had somehow brought a number of weeds with them. Al mostly slept and thought; Wiener cleaned the capsule from time to time and looked after the equipment which was jumbled on shelves built around the walls.

As a result of some error Dr. Irma had produced an infant shortly after the beginning of their fifth year in residence, a healthy but unnaturally intelligent girl now ten months old, who screamed continually in the bed cubicle despite her sensorially enriched environment. All the others slept in the laboratory. Irma had not yet forgotten her experience and grumbled constantly as she plodded through her daily chores, cooking, mending, and washing diapers, which hung cloyingly from every exposed pipe or wire. She seasoned the hydroponics under the floor with the dirty wash water.

"Shut up, you filthy brat!" she screamed, and Al eased himself to his feet and shuffled through the narrow door into the next room to quiet the baby. Wiener put down his knife and started to scratch listlessly around in the detritus on the floor in search of something to add to the child's sensory development collection. Everything in the laboratory cubicle had already been dismantled at least once and handed to the child to feel, shake or examine. But in vain; she seldom slept and was always bored.

Morale was at a low ebb, but not its lowest, for the evening would bring amusement in the form of a game of Bridge with some of the neighboring delegates, complete with refreshing argument, misunderstandings, threats, slamming of doors, closing of circuits or plugging of access holes in the walls. Without this variety and excitement in their lives the three of them felt they would not be able to stand their miserable existence.

There was an anticipatory thudding in the ceiling near one corner of the main room; it was the Rda who lived above them in an environment they had never seen, as they were unable to look through the pin hole which he used when visiting them. Wiener climbed up on a pile of cans and undid a small toggle screw in the ceiling. Instantly the room was filled with an invisible flurry and a rustling like dried leaves. The Rda metamorphosed before them and became an extremely long fuzzy metal-colored serpent already draped comfortably over salient parts of the room, in and out of pipes and coiled neatly here and there on the floor. His head was not visible for it had disappeared into the baby's cubicle. This was not unusual for he customarily visited the baby first; she was always fascinated by him and could now be heard gurgling contentedly.

Soon his head snaked in to greet his patiently waiting hosts. It was a triangular head with three piercing blue eyes set into the three points and a charming little three-cornered mouth in the middle. He lacked a nose, but there was no space for one.

"Good evening," he said in his low flute-like voice. He spoke perfect Bostonian, a language he had learned while residing in that city many years before. "I am early, but after our delightful game I will have to leave right away. I am needed in the bowels of the Imbalancia for some delicate adjustments in hard to reach places. You have probably noticed that I am shorter than usual this evening. Much of my past is coiled in my apartment out of harm's way, and I left about 80 centimeters with the charming infant to keep her quiet. I only require two segments to play Bridge and very few more to handle my duties on the Good Ship Out-of-Plumb; the rest of my length I brought for conversational purposes, to be witty, to match cleverness for cleverness, to be charming." He smiled sweetly at the three humans in turn, ending with Irma, over whose neck and waist he cast a friendly coil. "And

I keep some other segments by me in order to amuse myself with a few good memories during odd moments." Here he gave Irma an encouraging squeeze and then loosed her. Her down-turned mouth and clenched teeth relaxed slightly.

"Where is my good friend the Maximal Radial Thinker, so wise, so graceful, so multiple like a porcupine?" he asked rhetorically, darting his head over to the table, the only uncluttered surface in the room, at which the humans were accustomed to eat, write and play cards. He rested one of his apexes or chins upon the edge of the table and waited cheerfully for the cards to be dealt. His three antennae coiled and uncoiled in anticipation of receiving a good hand.

Al had turned on the loudspeaker attached to the intercom. A voice, seemingly struggling with bronchial pneumonia complicated by a plugged nose, choked out a loud "Ready." The men seated themselves and Al began to deal the cards. Then two long flexible tentacles, encased in black plastic sheaths emerged from two atmospheric protected vents in the wall just behind the table. They were about five feet long and ended in an eruption of twitching tips. They were burning hot, but the men were in no danger if they avoided contact and if the tentacles moved carefully and slowly. The twitching tips picked up a hand of cards without difficulty.

Bidding began with Al partnering the Rda and Wiener partnering their neighbor, the owner of the tentacles, who was the Radial delegate from Vpor. An unusual show of independence on Al's part made the Rda dummy for the first hand. He slithered away to talk with Irma, for whom he had a sentimental fondness, but she was already asleep on a pile of sacks filled with dried hydroponic weeds, snoring, a youthful expression on her prematurely aged face. He flexed his segments restlessly, which made him disappear and reappear from excursions into the past or future. The Radial and Wiener won the hand.

"Excuse me," gurgled Tak the Radial in his bubbly voice, and withdrew his chilled tentacles into his own apartment and replaced them with two fresh hot ones. The other players were quite used to seeing the venerable Radial change arms in midstream, and were careful to avoid the tentacle tips when they were newly hot as the slightest touch could raise blisters.

It was a relief to the two extraterrestrials when the slow hand of Bridge with the human players was over and they could really pit their skills against each other. Unlike the Rda, the Radial could not travel into the future, but he could extrapolate the course of the game with his multi-lobed brain, which he normally utilized to chart the course of the Imbalancia in its trips around the Universe, although the Earthlings did not know it. Nor did they know that the regular Bridge game was an act of condescension on the part of Tak, who could guess their moves in advance, and also of the Rda, who could remember them. Perhaps the aliens also were lonely in their protective isolation and had come to visit the other creatures in the "Zoo."

There was a sudden violent lurching in the capsule; all present fell except the Rda, a gurgle came from the loudspeaker, the cards were dispersed on the floor, and a stunned silence from the nursery was followed by an alarmed whimper. Dr. Irma leaped up and tore around the partition in maternal frenzy. Only the Rda remained calm.

"I will investigate," he said soothingly, and disappeared, possibly to travel through the pinhole into his apartment above and from there through more pinholes until he reached the cause of the commotion. His method of travel was the subject of much speculation among the humans who were confined to their cell.

Shortly after the cards had been retrieved from the floor Irma re-emerged with the quieted baby, who was clutching her two segments of the Rda like a living toy. The Rda segments looked exactly like the main Rda except they were shorter, and the one on top was engaged in telling her stories which made her chuckle. This was familiar sight to the humans, who were grateful that their lengthy guest was kind enough to donate parts of himself to keep the infant quiet.

The Rda reappeared and, taking back his two segments from the baby, reported that the ship had merely slowed down preparatory to landing at a new planet the following month.

"Our wet friend with the 'n' number of brains knew all about it, since he piloted the course," he said nastily as he bent over to kiss the baby in greeting. "But he has no memories at all except for a few in the oldest of his lobes; some of the new ones are just centimeters across and can only absorb a few seconds of stimulation. The storage areas tend to be undeveloped in the immature cells (an aging problem I believe). No basic integrity in the race." He glanced affectionately down his own lovely length. "Besides, the child might have been jarred out of bed and injured."

The Bridge game recommenced with new enthusiasm. Al was dummy this time. The Radial played his hand most brilliantly, and the Rda flicked his cards around with such speed that the humans could barely follow the movements for he was often a blur. Of course both of the extraterrestrials cheated, as was their custom, for no one had taught them the Golden Rule when they were young. The Rda was taking quick jaunts into the future to see which cards were going to be laid down, and Tak was consulting his Anebit pocket-piece whose perfect play-back bolstered his own faltering memory.

The desire to play tricks on the unsuspecting is a part of the extraterrestrial psyche. For example the Earthling's oxygen supply had failed several years earlier due to a bacteria infestation in the hydroponics; their amused neighbors had disconnected the system and had hitched the Earth cell up to the unending oxygen supply of the provident Imbalancia, not wanting to lose their Bridge partners. But they neglected to mention this to the humans. Thereafter they amused themselves watching Irma and Wiener making their futile daily rounds, encouraging the hydroponics and scrubbing the old air with endless filters, while in actuality their bad air was illegally flying out a vent and polluting the Universe. The Earthlings were not the only victims of these practical jokers; the ecological-minded "masters" were too.

But now the Titans of time, multiplicity and duplicity were locked in a battle to win the Bridge hand. The combined waves of mental concentration and annoyance set up such a powerful energy field in the room that Irma waded through it with difficulty as she put the baby to bed and stirred up a mess of greens, which she handed around on plates as a hydroponic snack. The guests declined but the men wolfed it down greedily.

A ticking inside one of the consoles indicated signs of instrument malfunction, a common enough outcome of a highly-charged Bridge game. Wiener cast aside his chair and darted to the injured instrument. Without his meticulous attention the equipment would have fallen into the same disrepair as the tape library for which Al had been responsible.

The ticking continued. Wiener adjusted a fine point, which began to trace lines on a vision tape. He stared at the lines in disbelief, gave a hoarse cry, and falling on his knees began to sob.

"God be praised! We're saved!" The others rushed to his side. The taco-grav was working! After six years of silence they were once again in contact with Earth.

It took a moment for this news to penetrate. Then Irma began to scold in a malicious and extremely loud voice.

"You'll see! You'll see!" she shrieked. "You'll see what they do to you! Both of you! Rape! Rape!" She began to laugh wildly. Al tried to restrain her to clam her down but she evaded him and stamped her feet in a paroxysm of rage until the Rda looped some coils around her in a python grip, which quieted her at once.

The message began to translate on the printer; it was not in Esperanto as they had expected but in Bostonian.

"Help!" stuttered the message. "We are lost. Where are we? Find our coordinates. Help!" the message went on and on repeating itself, the little needle copied its scratchy pattern endlessly, and the printer translator clattered. There was no indication of who was sending the message, just the continued plea for assistance. So many of the words were misspelled in the repetitions that they thought the message might have said something further, but with the help of Tak, who was watching through his spy hole and who narrowed down the possibilities with his multi-lobed brain, they could see that it was always the same.

It took the excited Wiener, Irma, the Radial and the Rda over seven hours to calculate the position of the sender, and they were only able to do so by unscrewing the taco-grav from the wall, and moving it about the room and calculating the timing of the impulses in different positions, a delicate and irritating process that delighted the Radial and no one else. Al alternately paced with the baby or brewed them green tea. The calculations were made much more difficult by the message continually stopping at one astral position and starting again at another.

They beamed a taco-grav message to the latest location and attempted to increase the likelihood of contact by randomly selecting areas in its vicinity for further contact, as suggested by the Radial. Their message was simple; they announced that they were sending from the Imbalancia and offered guidance and assistance to the lost crew. But there was no answer. The babble continued irritatingly from the same spot, which meant that the sender had come to rest somewhere.

"They must lack the proper equipment to receive us, or have broken it," sighed Tak. "We will try the next best thing. They are close enough for direct missiles to reach them; the Imbalancia has some heavy artillery we might be allowed to employ for compassionate purposes. It is better than letting the poor creatures die slowly in space." Radials are known for their kindness to family and dependents, and Tak was in an especially expansive and kindly mood because he had won the last five hands of Bridge.

But before the artillery could be requisitioned Al had solved the communications problem. Devoid of scientific talent or training, he had learned Morse code along with tent-pitching and fire-making during his years as a licensed Superior Child (second class), and desirous of displaying his control of the ether he insisted on trying to send a Morse code message. He drew up a bench importantly to the now reattached taco-grav and transmitted slowly by connecting and disconnecting the entire machine as it beamed a steady stream of anti-neutrinos at its target. The rude remarks of the others ceased suddenly when there was an answer from what must have been another licensed Superior Child.

"Hello. Thank goodness there is someone there who can send an intelligible message in Bostonian. Direct us to you, or come to us. This is Fastar LBR-210663871. We are on an asteroid without water or atmosphere. Though still operant, we are low on fuel. I am Dr. Eustacia Fish, M.D., chief of Classified Experimental Re-adaptation Project RES 00543.7, carrying a valuable cargo, lost on my way to RES lab headquarters on the Imbalancia and demanding assistance."

"What is RES?" Al asked her.

"Relocation of Endangered Species" was the reply. "A new branch at the Imbalancia. There seems to be considerable lack of organized communication between governmental agencies. The guide lists must be out of date again. We at RES attempt to modify biological structures to fit existing or available environments. My project involves adapting life-forms to an alcohol-based planet. The MES on the other hand, or Maintenance of Endangered Species, seeks to maintain or improve environments instead of modifying the species to fit existing conditions. Another branch, the CES, or Collection of Endangered Species, though fully licensed by the Aubudon Society, as are the RES and the MES, functions mainly as voyeurs and has no protective instincts at all. They are merely historians and curators."

It was obvious that Dr. Eustacia Fish had been a Very Superior Child. Al had considerable difficulty keeping up with her even though he was the possessor of the advanced Morse badge.

"I would not be surprised if the malfunction of our Fastar and the abortion of our mission were caused by agents of the CES concealed in the Fastar construction plant, or by the MES, both of whom could have deliberately miscalculated our trajectory. They will hear about this. I believe the MES will stop at nothing to prove that Relocation of Endangered Species is not the only practical means of species protection, and are willing to waste valuable lives and equipment to show the Aubudon Society that the RES is unproductive and expensive. I will complain to the proper authorities at the Imbalancia. Put me in touch with them now."

There was an embarrassed pause while Al attempted to

construct an answer that would not reveal the delegates' total lack of communication with or even knowledge of the authorities, and at the same time hide their inability to save the Doctor and her valuable cargo. Providing directions for the Fastar to travel to the Imbalancia would be fruitless in view of its limited fuel, even if they had known how to direct its pre-set programs. All three humans pleaded with Tak and the Rda for help, each after his own fashion, meanwhile beaming messages back to the alarmed Dr. Fish that help was on its way.

It was Irma who finally convinced the Radial by loud threats that she would die in her next confinement, when there was a doctor so near and yet so far. She pointed out that the result of such a tragedy would be that the other humans would have to raise both babies, and that would be the end of the Bridge games.

Tak reluctantly promised to communicate with the control unit of the Imbalancia and attempt to have fuel and directions shipped to the lonely asteroid. The Radial withdrew his arms, his gurgling voice was heard no more, and the anxious delegates were forced to repress their curiosity and wait.

THE FASTAR

About three weeks later the Imbalancia settled down on the new planet. A few days after that, while Irma's arms were up to her elbows in diapers and murky water, there was a horrible crash and everything went black. The port hole was darkened by a large body which had slammed into the side of the cell. Eagerly they turned on the artificial lighting, and looking through the dark window saw a small metal door no larger than the port itself. Then a deafening grinding and booming jarred the whole cell for several minutes. When the noise had stopped they heard Tak's voice croaking from the loudspeaker, which had been on continuously since the night of the Bridge party.

"You may open your port hole now. Atmospheric conditions are equalized between the two cells. The robots have made a tight join."

Wiener unscrewed the port eagerly. They waited, but the metal door of the Fastar remained tightly closed. They knocked on the door with Al's copper pipe and received a response in clanging tones to match theirs. From the rhythm it appeared to be Morse code again, and translations were irritably recommenced.

No, the door was not stuck. Dr. Fish would not open it. She had valuable life-forms in there as well as herself. As a medical doctor she found it her duty and in the best interest of her shipment to declare the Imbalancia in quarantine for ten days. At the end of which time, if she were satisfied that they did not carry diseases that would harm her or her companions, for whom she was solely responsible and for whom she had signed receipts, and if she could receive assurances that the delegates really were whom they said they were, she would open the door.

"Do you have a small drill?" asked the Rda, who had appeared and was watching intently. Wiener offered him a choice of bits from the repair bulkhead and fitted one into an electric drill. After a few seconds of drilling into what might have been the thinnest part of the door, the bit snapped; the metal was too strong for their light tools.

The door began to vibrate with new taps from inside and the tedious business of taking messages began again. Dr. Fish had guessed what they were up to and was angry.

"How about a little acid?" suggested the Rda. Accordingly some Sulfuric acid was applied to a spot where a mild indentation suggested the possible presence of a hinge. But since the surface was vertical the acid ran down and they were rewarded with nothing more than a hideous smell.

News of what was happening must have penetrated to the visitors, for the next Morse message read: "All inhabitants of our vessel with the exception of resistant plant life have received immunization against a new strain of Staphylococcus included in our cargo. Not a fatal infection, but painful and long-lasting. I am prepared to retaliate."

"Bug-off!" replied Al, not forgetting to add the exclamation point.

"I am responsible for four fellow humans and valuable equipment for an alcohol adaption program," was the dignified reply. A little cover flipped open in the upper part of the door; it was a peephole. A blue eye glared at them. The owner of the eye tapped, "Please take blood smears from all of you and hold them up to this viewer so they may be scanned. We shall taco-grav Earth at once to establish your genotypes and identities. And be sure that any more infringement of our privacy rights will be reported at the same time. Not only do we rely upon our constitutionally guaranteed right to privacy, but we have a Prince of the Blood as part of our cargo. He is destined to be a Delegate-at-Large."

They obligingly stuck themselves to get blood samples, with the exception of the Rda who had no blood. Evidently Dr. Fish was able to contact Earth, for which they were thankful, for their own Taco-grav stubbornly refused to work properly and they dearly wanted to send a shopping list of items to be included in the next supply ship.

There was nothing to do but wait. The Fastar was closely sealed; the Rda had tunneled outside to verify this. He had no need of a space suit and was equally at home in oxygen, ammonia or anything else, as he never breathed and never ate, so far as his human companions could determine. He had slipped inside the visiting Fastar somehow and found it in the same good condition as when it had left Earth. It was a fine new expensive model, and except for lack of fuel, it was ready to take off again.

However, the fuel tanks did not seem very large. They had probably not been prepared for a lengthy journey or for getting lost, which would explain the break-down on the asteroid, but further calculations convinced him that the tanks had not originally been large enough for a round trip to the Imbalancia. Had the Fastar perhaps been meant to remain permanently at its destination? Or never to arrive? He resolved not to mention this possibility to the delegates.

They prepared to wait the full ten days in frustration, with no other communication than polite twice daily inquiries to confirm each other's continued existence. Half-way through the eighth day, while the delegates were seated at their mid-day meal, they heard a loud hiss and a thud from the direction of the port hole. They looked over to see the upper half of a young woman protruding through the opening. She was round-cheeked with large green eyes, and her breasts, which were huge and clad in stretched white knitted material, protruded well into the room. Her hair was red and curly.

"Good morning, you guys!" she said cheerily. "It's all right, Doctor," she called over her shoulder and drew back into the Fastar.

A different white-clad form appeared at the porthole, and shortly afterwards a long leg dangled out of it, as far as the thigh. It was clad in white satin spray and an elegant red shoe with a spring heel, Irma noted with a pang. Another leg sought to enter and after undergoing some contortions managed to do so. Then both legs turned their backs and slid in, followed by a rump encased in white panties, a wrinkled white dress and the rest of a disheveled blond young woman. She turned to face them with a glare.

"Dr. Livingstone, I presume," said Wiener before he could stop himself.

"Dr. Eustacia Fish," hissed the newcomer.

Irma advanced with considerable dignity, introduced herself as head of the delegation and offered its friendship and assistance, such as they were, to the new arrivals. Their hospitality was available to the utmost, as were their instruments and advice. The delegates would in return be grateful for the use of the newcomers' taco-grav. Now perhaps a hydroponic snack to begin with? Dr. Fish refused the food; they had their own ample supplies. "Perhaps some vitamins and minerals for yourself?" she suggested, eyeing Irma's expanded waistline.

"And the other members of your party?" asked Irma curiously, trying not to peer shamelessly into the Fastar beyond the port hole.

"I have a subject and two nurses, Miss Squieze and Miss Constable. They will do very well where they are. Also a passenger, a Delegate-at-Large. An important young personage, Robert the Bruce, Hereditary Prince of the Americas. He is making an educational tour of the Aubudon Society and has letters of introduction to the authorities. You are to address him as 'Prince' and to facilitate his movements in every way. You can come out now, Prince," she cooed.

A pale young man, sickly looking and dressed in a dirty white coverall, stuck the upper half of his body into the room. His face was thin and the hair on his scalp and chin was patchy. The scaling effect was enhanced by pale blotchy freckles and spots of acne. His eyes were red-rimmed and unfocused.

"No!" shouted Dr. Fish "Get back inside, Harp! I want the Prince!"

The young man who next slid out of the port hole was very different. His coverall was new and bright red, adorned here and there with gold piping. A wide striped ribbon hung around his neck with a jeweled ornament that flapped inconveniently. His physique was excellent and his face was handsome with a broad chin punctuated by a dimple. He greeted the delegates gracefully, putting them at their ease as only an affable prince can. They quickly unloaded his belongings which included a good supply of delicacies that made their mouths water.

Dr. Fish showed no surprise when the baby revealed her presence by beginning to yell. She ignored the existence of the two men delegates, since Irma had failed to introduce them. The Rda probably passed as insulated piping. Everything that Dr. Fish was willing to see in the cell was soon seen. It suddenly looked sordid to its inhabitants as she gazed around with politely expressionless eyes. She seemed somewhat interested in their communications equipment and dwindling supply of chemicals and she lowered herself down the trap to take a quick look at the hydroponics, which were in abundant slushy bloom. The baby got a cursory look and a poke while she inquired as to her name and date of birth. Irma was unable to supply an answer to either question. All the while the Doctor maintained a haughty expression as though there were some unpleasant odor in the room, which there was, of course, due to the necessary recycling of all their wastes through the garden and the tendency of the trap door to jam open a little.

Then she invited Irma to step into the Fastar with her, which was accomplished by building a set of steps out of tin cans and by boosting and persuading. As soon as the two women were inside, the door slammed shut.

Brute settled comfortably in Al's arm chair to watch any developments. Al and Wiener waited uneasily for more than an hour, passing around meaningless remarks. They agreed that the girls would probably want to talk, and that it probably would do

Irma good. But the baby could only be placated by feeding and its only food was what Irma carried about her, although the infant was sometimes willing to dribble strained hydroponics. Preliminary squawks came from the baby's room. Wiener quickly strained some of the leafy mess; the baby spat it out and yelled. They attempted to open the door into Dr. Fish's Fastar, but they knew it would be locked. Wiener held the child while Al laid out Bridge hands.

"For God's sake, call the Rda!" shouted Wiener, who broke first. But then the door suddenly opened and the buxom nurse leaned out.

"May I have the baby, please?" She was handed over gladly and the door closed behind her.

This time the period of waiting was much shorter. The three men had scarcely started polite fencing and boasting, the prelude to sharing their histories and opinions, when the door opened and the baby was handed back, clean and quiet. Then the door shut again. The baby was unable to tell them what was going on in the Fastar, so they laid her back in her damp bed where she went to sleep.

In their anxiety they tried to call the Rda by banging on the ceiling, which was no help, and then knocked on the Radial's window for assistance in locating the Rda. They were much hampered in this process by Brute, who ran back and forth asking questions.

The Rda rustled into view. "So sorry to delay. But I have been having a most pleasant time inside the ventilation system of our visitor's Fastar. Allow me to tell you; it will make you chuckle. It is much like the interior of a shop for pets, such as used to be found on your Earth in the old days when it was still fully civilized. There is a large turtle upon which the feet are rested, as on a footstool; the walls are covered with cages containing birds, serpents, rodents and cactus plants. Occupying much of the floor are cages, one containing a monkey of a hairy sort with a tail, and another containing a human appearing animal wearing clothes."

"That's just Harp," explained Brute. "He must have gotten wild again. Most of the time they let him roam."

There is also a cat which sleeps on the doctor's bed. The bed has coverings similar to that which the Helio Monster, whose body I was inhabiting on my last trip to Earth, tore to pieces in a hotel. They have also brought ample provisions of every kind, which they mean to share with you. They have only a limited supply of hydroponic matter, so you must share yours with them. There is a machine to wash clothes. How amusing! The females were talking among themselves when I slipped away, and Irma was describing you two in unfriendly terms. She did not mention myself. That was disappointing for I was looking forward to suddenly appearing before them at the sound of my name."

At that point the connecting door flew open and Harp wiggled through rapidly yet reluctantly, as though he were being propelled from behind.

"They don't want me," he mumbled apologetically. Miss Squieze's head appeared behind him.

"Mind you don't give him anything to eat or drink, the doctor says, nothing at all. Shall I repeat?"

"Of course, of course," said Wiener impatiently, paying no attention to what she had told them, only disconcerted by the sight of all her voluptuous flesh put to no use. The door slammed shut once again.

"Give me water, for God's sake!" whined Harp. "I need something to eat, too." His eyes darted around greedily. He had exceptionally bad breath and his teeth were coated with a sticky film. There was pus in the corner of one eye.

"I can't. Doctor's orders. You're sick," said Al kindly. "I don't know what the result would be."

The youth began to giggle. "I'd grow wings. I'd fly. Straight up into the air." He began to flap his arms to show them, laughing at the way they dodged in the small room. Then he began to cry, and kneeling, wrapped his hands around Wiener's legs and kissed his feet in their dirty cloth slippers.

"Give the boy some water," a voice gargled from the loud

speaker; the Radial had been listening.

"Give him nothing of the sort," said Dr. Fish distinctly from the door, which had opened again. "He is an experimental subject and I am responsible for him. Water might be fatal. He has been ejected from our quarters temporarily during my examination of Dr. Scriema, but we will take him back one half hour from now and replace him in his cage. I am sorry he has caused you inconvenience."

"Don't let her get me," wailed Harp. He had a long flexible tube protruding from the back of one hand. The area around it was red and swollen; his lips were caked and had cracked recently, for there was new blood over the old.

"He can stay here," offered Al and Wiener at the same time.

"Very well. We will take him in at feeding time with the baby, and return them both when we are finished. He is quite nasty to have around, I will admit." She had not noticed the Rda though she was looking right at him. Al and Wiener now saw her clearly for the first time. She had an extraordinary beauty; there was also an extraordinary look of hostility in her eyes. "Your acceptance of him is appreciated. It will make things much more comfortable for Dr. Scriema."

"May we talk to her?" asked Al eagerly.

"You may not. And I doubt she will speak to either of you, or so she has given me to understand. If she changes her mind I will let you know."

"Is she in labor?" asked Wiener, the familiar terror rising in his chest.

"Certainly not." The door slammed shut.

The boy did seem to be ill. He lay down on Irma's sack and fell asleep. The baby was asleep too in her bed behind the wall. The Rda had treated her to clean sheets; someone in the Fastar had washed her hair and it fluffed up in blond fuzz. Her nose was clean for a change. The three men tiptoed to the side of the room as far away from the two sleepers as possible and turned down the loudspeaker which was close at hand. The Rda joined the conference.

Irma was clearly a hostage. And the boy, whom they held, was obviously of little comparable value.

"This is indeed a disagreeable and difficult female doctor," gargled Tak. "I hear of the work of her department from time to time. There is some disagreement within the Aubudon Society as to the proper handling of Endangered Species. I, myself, and my people too, believe in some moderate relocation. But we consider biological adaptation as too extreme and often destructive; we predict that on a large scale it will decimate the remains of small populations. So I am glad to see that this female scientist has only limited samples on which to experiment. The scientific community will naturally ignore her skimpy findings, so she will not be much of a danger."

Brute listened with close attention, while the others had heard this speech before.

"Nor can I look with approval on the anti-relocation party, or the PES. Their efforts to change or adapt the surroundings of the species for its protection are inimical to the natural evolution of the environment itself, and are basically against the tenets of the Aubudon Society; Such advocates are sliding swiftly into Stasis and Ultra Conservatism."

"And what do you call it if in your zeal you collect an entire population without providing it any scraps of its natural habitat, nor encouraging it to adapt to a new environment?" asked the Rda smoothly, shifting from the rapid hissing language in which he generally spoke with Tak, into slow Bostonian in order to make himself intelligible to the humans.

"An activity of the collection department, and on a destructive scale. I and my people are unalterably opposed to the collectors of the CES," said Tak firmly. "Take the classic examples of the foolish earth inhabitants. They once collected bird's eggs as ornaments, and seal skins to wear, thus decimating more than one population. Their punishment was swift; their descendants have suffered plague after plague of cockroaches and gold fish, which now threaten their existence. As for you, during your universal travels you must have seen punishments meted out to those who change the Universe for their own pleasure."

"Indeed," said the Rda. "I once visited an asteroid at the outermost limits of the Universe and found that the nearest source of nutrinos had dried up due to a nova brought on by careless prospecting. That was an anxious moment; I became so thin that I nearly broke apart prematurely. But we were speaking of collectors of endangered species. What should one think of a people that collects an entire species and keeps it caged?"

"Shocking."

"Caged, so to speak, in their waistcoat pockets; thus depriving it of the right to adapt itself and reproduce?"

"In the first place," roared Tak, "You cannot prove that the Anebit is a living creature!"

"Send it home to Alaphat and find out!" roared the Rda in return.

"Some other race will seize them if we do. They are defenseless. We love them. We help them. At least we keep them warm and in good health. We even educate them."

"And send one of them to serve as a delegate for its race to the Imbalancia?"

"Not exactly as a delegate. Yes, I admit there is one on board at the present time. The personal pocket piece of my great uncle Tak."

"Which he has lent to you, no doubt. It is probably in your pocket right now. And though it is not really alive, you have trained it very well to play Bridge. I notice that your game has improved since you have been cheating with the aid of the Anebit's convenient memory."

There was a snap and a flash of light as the loud speaker went dead.

"What are you talking about?" asked Wiener.

"Our damp friend has just realized that I have been in the habit of spying upon his actions," simpered the Rda. "He thought his heat seal would keep me out. But this simple ectomorph does not realize that I have only to go forward to the time when he is dead and his home is unlocked, slip in, go back to the present time, look into his Anebit where he has codified all the habitual moves of his Bridge opponents, then fly forward quick as a flash, pop back into this room and return to the present moment. It will take him a little while to figure it out and take precautions."

"Oh," laughed Brute, "You have both been cheating!" As a prince he had never found it necessary to mince words.

"But what is an Anebit?" asked Wiener placatingly.

"A creature from Alaphat, a planet with nothing but oil, igneous rocks and silicone in suspension. It used to be inhabited by Anebits until the Radials 'explored' it during a period when the Aubudon Society was busy preventing World War III on Earth The Radials are an emotional people, and for some unknown reason they thought they had to have an Anebit to carry around with them in their pockets. They decimated the population, by taking them back home with them to Vpor, where most of the little creatures died from overheating. Tak's great uncle was one of the original explorers. The poor thing is now many thousands of years old and has retired to Vpor to lie stupidly in the steam, with most of his lobes rotted away. Tak is only half as old and is still an active Major Thinker. He keeps his uncle's toy carefully in a refrigerator most of the time. The Anebits are getting rarer and rarer, as they refuse to breed in captivity. Tak would never be able to maintain his position as navigator of the Imbalancia without the Anebit to assist his poor memory; otherwise he would only be a humble delegate like ourselves. He gets to do anything he wants and even has his own traveldrop to use whenever he wishes to leave the Imbalancia."

"But I thought Tak said the Anebits were not alive."

"They may look like a computer and act like a computer, but they are very much alive and have a brain and a great deal of temperament. They have a single eye and remember everything they see if they choose to open the lid that shelters it. If anyone tries to open the lid for them they either bite him by snapping it shut, or if terribly offended, self-destruct in a puddle of oil and bits of silicone. Otherwise they live almost forever. They look a bit like flattened red rubber balls, not unlike those infant Radials back on Vpor, which they call jelly pups, and like them they insist on being tickled on the tummy; though in the case of the Anebit you cannot tell front from back, though some maintain that the hinge of the lid is toward the back."

"But how can it act like a computer?" persisted Wiener.

"If you are able to look into its lid you will see its eye and two little spots or buttons. Do not attempt to press them. You may ask it anything you want, since it understands all languages, even silent ones, and it will answer if it chooses by flashing the two little buttons on and off in a binial language which the Radials are well equipped to understand. I sat with it once in its refrigerator while Tak was asleep, and with a good deal of persuasion I got it to open its lid. He keeps it cheaply, stored with his perishable foods, and gives it a little flax seed oil from time to time."

At this point Al remember that he had not tasted the delicacies that had come with the Prince and hinted that it was time for dinner. The nurse appeared at the Fastar's door and they handed up Harp and the baby, then settled down to the best meal the delegates had eaten in six years. The Rda did not stay, as the sight of human food disgusted him. He disappeared through his pinhole, perhaps to look in on other unsuspecting delegates.

Afterwards, having taken Harp and the baby back again and put them both to bed, the men lay replete and conversed about the things they had seen and heard. Brute deferred to Al who was bigger, and to Wiener who was smarter, and so they enjoyed their alternative conversations and snoozes punctuated by necessary inspections of the equipment and exchanges of Harp and the baby, who gave them little trouble, even though Irma did not appear again. They missed her, of course, but life on the whole was satisfying. Sometimes they would hear the Rda talking or singing or hissing to the baby behind her partition and occasionally she responded in kind. They ate delicious things out of cans while the baby and Harp were provided for in the Fastar. Harp would wake up from time to time and complain, but he could be quieted with surreptitious drinks of water and a little food. The conversation was enlivening; on the whole the delegates forgot that Brute was a prince.

But one morning he crawled out from his comfortable sleeping bag with its automatically controlled pneumatic mattress, and after stretching, brought the idyl to a halt by announcing that the time had come to present his credentials to the head of the Aubudon Society.

"This has all been a lot of fun, guys. But it's getting a little dull. Time for me to go to work!"

THE NEW PLANET

After days of the jarring, booming and continual rat-tatting of the robots, the Imbalancia was finally settled into position for the Aubudon Society's next planetary inspection. On some previous planets the inmates of the Earth cubicle had watched the settling-in process through their port hole, but this time the window was not available, and they were denied the noisy pleasure of watching the robots crawl out of their crannies in the sides of the great ship, pull down the landing pods, and commence their structural and cosmetic repairs.

The offended Tak had withdrawn himself but when Wiener buzzed him on the prince's behalf he quickly responded, his anger forgotten. Surprisingly he also responded to his Highness's demand to be conducted to the Aubudon leadership. A neat little compression chamber appeared in the wall next to the sink after only a couple of hours of banging by the service robots. They found four rather badly fitting space suits piled inside and tried them on. But only one had connections to a portable oxygen tank, so Brute helped himself to that one and with his credentials safely tucked inside he shut himself into the air lock. Soon afterwards they heard him slam the outside door. Since there were no communication devices inside the suits, Al and Wiener had no idea what became of him.

His departure was not a total loss; it had been too crowded in the cubicle and the prince tended to talk incessantly. His short acquaintance with both science and political economy, the only subjects of real interest to the others, did not prevent him from holding forth. By listening to their lectures his knowledge had improved quite a bit but still he was annoying.

Harp, who knew almost nothing and was unteachable, gave them less trouble, though sometimes they had to climb over him to get around the room, his breath smelled bad, and they had to wake him whenever Miss Squieze came for him and the baby. But then he was always willing to fetch the baby out of bed and hand her up to the nurse as she leaned out through the port hole.

Had it not been for the care of the baby, the cooking and the extra labor of weeding the hydroponics falling upon the men, they might not have missed Irma and her scolding at all, so dazzled were they by the friendly and buxom nurse who frequently stopped to chat with them. She had not yet ventured into the room but leaned farther in as time went on. It was expected that some day she would lose her balance and fall through, and they predicted she would have great difficulty getting out again.

It was during this period that the new baby was born. Dr. Fish did not bother to reveal the news to the men, so the only word they had on such an important event was the report of the Rda who had watched the proceedings with great interest. It was a boy, and very ugly. He remained in the Fastar with his mother and it did not look as though the two of them intended to return in the near future.

Filled with boredom and frustration of every kind the men contacted Tak, with whom they were again on speaking terms, and begged him to get them permission to join the planet inspection team, which in this case was a delegation of quartz-plated walking plants and cocci-type hoppers, both of whom needed no protective suits or warmth in the nitrogen and CO-2 rich atmosphere that Tak told them was the ambience of the planet.

Wiener and Al gladly donned space suits, which they found were now complete with the appropriate hoses and oxygen tanks. They had never walked in space suits before; in the past they had satisfied their curiosity through the port hole.

The Rda accompanied them on their excursion. As usual he

had no need for protective clothing or artificial life supports. After some argument they also took Harp in the smaller suit intended for Irma. It would have been preferable to leave him and his alternating noisy or silent despair behind with the baby, but as the planet was reputed to contain alcohol he had been ordered out by Dr. Fish for an acclimatizing walk. Though it would be years before he could be physically exposed, the contact might do him some psychological good and he would also serve to transport other life-forms on their own acclimatizing tour: a number of glass bottles containing green and red algae were suspended from wires slung across his back and chest, where they slopped in their solutions, only protected from spillage by filter paper tops, some tied on with cotton thread and some with silk.

"I wonder if there will be any water out there," ventured Harp. He had been given sugared agar before leaving and was almost coherent for a change. The others viewed him with their usual disgust, but also with increased interest.

"You have to remember that water is not good for you," said Al in a kindly voice, recalling very well that when he had given the boy pieces of wet green slush he had sucked greedily at them and it had not seemed to do him any harm. But it was not profitable to anger Dr. Fish.

They crowded themselves into the tiny vestibule, shut one door, waited a while, opened the other, and slid down a chute onto the planet's surface.

The inspectors had already potted some large plants which were now resting in containers of solution, or in large tubs of colorful soil, all standing on motorized dollies. Some of the researchers were grouped around a hefty cactus-like plant of a brilliant green color and were examining it carefully. The cactus drew into itself a little and ejected a dangerous looking spine at one of the researchers, who, however, was too fast for it and caught the missile neatly on a hard shining scale. At this sign of aggression other investigators wiggled or leapt out of open cells in the skin of the giant ship and converged on their hostile and perhaps intelligent find, which was possibly of sufficient caliber to become a delegate itself.

From without the Imbalancia looked more like a blasted asteroid than an efficient space ship; somewhat like a bruised pudding stone. The mouths of the open cubicles resembled craters and a steamy substance or gas floated out of some of them. Cells of all shapes and sizes clung to the outside and to each other like limpets, or dangled in strings like bacteria; if any part of the ship's original hull had been visible the men would not have recognized it as such. Everything was space-worn and colorless except for Dr. Fish's Fastar and a few homes of other newcomers, which still bore traces of their original design.

Their own home was a rusty irregular blob with a chute sticking out of it. Dr. Fish's Fastar was a natty looking shark-shaped vehicle, built for show and for short solar flights. It had wings emblazoned on its sides, a fishtail at the back and a star plastered on its nose. Except where it was fastened to their cell by its door, neat port holes decorated its body at regular intervals. There was an ingenious observation bubble on the roof. But the inhabitants would never be able to see out again, as the voyage had pitted the Earth-manufactured ports until they were opaque. It looked like a ruined toy. Aware that they were invisible to the inhabitants, they examined the Fastar at their leisure and without embarrassment. It would bring hardly any cash in the second-hand market back on Earth in its present condition.

There was little else in the neighborhood to occupy their attention, nothing but the space ship with its pitted sides and another much smaller travel-worn black ship which lay a short distance from the Imbalancia. To be sure there were the potted plants under investigation and the peculiar looking investigators for them to stare at under the colorless sky, which was made more colorless still by the men having to look through their sight-dimming, surely second-hand plastic helmets. Wiener made a few mental notes of botanical eccentricities to be recorded on his return, and he snapped off a few specimens poking out from the pebbles beneath his feet and tucked them under his belt buckle, knowing full well that it was against the rules of the Society to do so. The ground was covered by pebbles of all sizes, colors and textures. Harp picked up a clumsy handful, but having no pocket to store them in, let them dribble out of his gloved fingers.

"Hmmm," said Wiener learnedly, "Quartz. It looks as though water has been here, signs of glaciers." For the suits were now fitted up with little radios worked by buttons, so they could communicate faintly with one another.

At first they thought that they must be the only creatures in space suits, but soon noticed a few other odd shapes sliding out of their doors and gliding down chutes; one awkward creature was actually disdaining his chute and flying down to the ground, a clumsy form flapping inside its suit and landing with a thump. Al thought that Brute might be out there somewhere and shouted for him, but little sound carried through his helmet.

They stared hopefully at the heavy black hulk of the smaller ship. It was at least two hundred feet long, resting on its own pods within easy walking distance of the Imbalancia. But it was featureless and closed, so they could not guess what class of creature inhabited it.

Their attention was then drawn to a shining multi-faceted vehicle clinging to the Imbalancia on the underpart of its body just above the point where the great ship rested on its powerful landing pods, which formed a dark colonnade beneath it. The vehicle was near enough to the ground for them to study it from where they stood below and to see themselves reflected distortingly on its curved lower surfaces. It must have been a recent arrival, for though the mirror work was dented here and there the journey through space had not spoiled its slick finish. It seemed to be a ship from a civilization advanced in technology far beyond that of Earth, and the men had an uneasy feeling that they were being observed through its walls and floor.

The black stranger ship was close enough for Al to see its distorted hulk also reflected in the mirrored surface. Suddenly the black ship and the Imbalancia seemed to him like an egg lying beside a giant lizard which had given it birth. The idea began to interest him, and he toyed with it; so rarely did he see anything unusual enough to stimulate his imagination. He tried to place their own tiny reflected forms into the metaphor; they were lice underneath the lizard, perhaps. Fleas? He hopped experimentally, watching his reflection in the mirror above, and then remembered that he might be under observation. He saw the four of them as tiny crushable creatures through what he thought might be the eyes of the observers above. The men probably looked as absurd to other life-forms as the Rda did to them, for he no longer had illusions about the attractiveness of the human form in alien eyes. For the first time Al saw himself with the mind of an ecologist.

He looked at his companions and noticed that the Rda was no longer at his side; the three men were alone. But there had been four little images reflected in the mirror. He looked up again, straining his neck to bring the eye-piece of his awkward helmet into position, and saw that the forth figure was a space-suited biped standing on the other side of the nearest pod, invisible to them below but apparent in the mirrored surface above.

As though the interloper had sensed his gaze, it began to travel at an ungainly trot toward the Black Ship. Al rounded the sheltering pod as fast as he could and was just in time to see the creature slip behind the Black Ship's landing gear, where it was lost from view.

Wiener and Harp had followed him out of curiosity, and he tried to communicate this mystery to them by gesticulation and running up and down, for their communication system was now almost inaudible. The others obediently circled the Black Ship, one clockwise and the other counter clockwise, with Al standing guard, but they found nothing. The interloper had either been swallowed by the ship above or had run on and was now crouched behind a landing pod, perhaps watching them with a weapon at the ready.

They did however find a surprising earth-artifact lying on the ground next to one of the Black Ship's landing struts. It was an excellent photograph measuring about 5x7 inches, nicely matted, depicting in full color a kind of long haired wispy green seaweed intertwined with thick ribbons of dark brown kelp, both

63

floating on the top of a gently foaming pale green wave with darker hollows beneath. The plant study was artistically composed with terrestrial sea boulders, and there were glimpses of pale blue sky. It was a nostalgic sight and Wiener picked it up carefully.

Communication having become urgent they walked back to their cell, depressurized in the tiny vestibule and returned to their normal clothing. Al told them of his discovery that there must be fellow humans on the planet. There was the prince, to be sure, but he did not walk like the stranger. They thought the interloper must be an illegal; otherwise he would have approached his fellow humans and identified himself.

"After all," said Wiener indignantly, "Our position as delegates is official. We should be the only humans here!"

"Dr. Fish and the nurses, though human, aren't actually delegates, though they did let us know of their arrival," argued Al. "Perhaps there are some other scientific teams like them on the Imbalancia, studying something." Al and Wiener had been stranded in space for such a long time that they usually took opposite sides in any discussion, merely to keep the conversation going.

But they were both nervous. The stranger seemed to be connected to a ship many times larger than their little cell, and there could be many more like him. Worse, the delegates had no weapons to defend themselves, and they had never seen any sign of a security force which they might call on for protection. Harp, on the other hand, was happy to consider interlopers, for any novel situation appeared more promising than his present one.

The Rda had left them during the early part of their walk and had not returned, for they pounded on his corner of the ceiling without result. They tried to contact the Radial but his communicator only buzzed. It was partly frightening though also exhilarating to contemplate a fight; it reminded them that they were responsible for the women and children, too. Al wandered over to the door leading to the baby's cubicle to see why she was not crying. The reason for the silence was immediately evident: the clumsy crib was empty, she was not there. His alarmed shout brought Wiener at a run.

"Irma's got her," he proposed soothingly. But there was no kicked over pile of cans below the door into the Fastar, and without the cans to serve as steps they knew that no member of either party could have squeezed through the port hole.

"Perhaps the baby suddenly learned to crawl," said Al hopefully. But a rapid search revealed no child hidden in any space large enough to contain one. They opened bulkheads at full speed and failed to close them, dragging clothes and supplies out of cupboards. An attempt was made to draw back the cover of the hydroponic well but it appeared to be finally stuck.

"Why not ask the nurse?" offered Harp. "Bang on the door."

"No. Wait a minute," Al waved down the suggestion. "Better not get her excited. Just act normal."

"She was kidnaped probably," Harp said with thinly disguised relish.

"Don't be more foolish than absolutely necessary," remarked Al nastily, barely avoiding kicking him as he lay comfortably on Irma's sack bed, eating salted peanuts.

"There is some logical explanation, of course," said Wiener. "We only have to find it." He squatted down on some of the scattered clothing and hung his chin thoughtfully on his chest while he cogitated. He asked the others for input and produced the following list:

1. The baby's mother did (or did not) have her. As there was no finding out, since questioning Irma would produce an irreversible interruption to their logical exploration, Al wished to examine the latter premise. But Wiener did not want to avoid the former without examining its possibilities, so:

2 (a) Assuming that she did have the baby, would she return her? (Or not?) This proved to be, on discussion, too speculative a path of conjecture and so they went on to consider:

2 (b) Assuming that she did not have the baby and that the child was incapable of independent locomotion she was in some other kind of friendly (or unfriendly) hands.

3 (ba) If in friendly hands there was no reason for anything but joy. But they were not disposed to be joyful, so they went on to examine the darker possibilities:

4 (bb) If in unfriendly hands, was the kidnaping for profit (or not)?

5 (bba) If for profit they were dealing with bribeable beings.

6 (bbb) If not for profit they were dealing with non bribeable beings. These beings could be divided into terrestrial or non-terrestrial creatures.

Wiener snatched a pencil and a scrap of paper. He began to put together a mathematical program, feeling that the complexity of the problem would soon necessitate super-human aid.

Harp was now chewing a piece of dried hydroponics topped with a slab of milk chocolate and following the argument as well as he could. "If we can pay them off it doesn't matter if they're human or not," he interjected. "Let's get those suits back on and find out what they want. They might be crazy or something and want to eat the kid, so we'd better get moving. It's them goons in the black ship. No telling what people will eat when they've been out in space long enough. Or maybe Earth's been taken over by aliens and the kids's one of the hostages."

Wiener, clinging to his notes, said the mathematical probabilities appeared to be greater that the creature (or creatures) were extra-terrestrial, but that he could not give the exact odds until he had the program finished. However, Al agreed with Harp that action was in order and they out voted Wiener two-to-one.

They began to dress again in their space suits, which was always a slow process, like knights donning armor. Harp disentangled the dangling bottles of plant samples from his suit. First he glanced suspiciously at the closed door of the Fastar, then tore the top off one bottle and after finishing out the greenery, drank off the remaining mixture of salt water, alcohol and soil nutrients. Still hungry, he opened another bottle and swigged the contents, weeds and all. He gagged a bit but was able to hold the mess down. He laid the other bottles aside.

Within a half hour they were out on the colorful pebbles of the planet surface again, this time with workable radio transenders from Wiener's instrument shelf. Harp was only equipped with a receiving unit, it being felt that they could do without his advice.

Night was about to fall, the first night that Al and Wiener had seen in years. The now yellow sky was turning gray and the legs of the Imbalancia cast long shadows on the speckled ground. The giant ship loomed above and it gave them a small feeling of security that they, official members of the ship's assembly, were bound on a lawful excursion to regain what was surely, even in extra-terrestrial circles, lawfully theirs. But the Imbalancia was silent and even the mirror-finished construction they had stood beneath earlier had ceased to shine and looked blind and opaque.

They paced slowly up and down the near side of the ship; it would have taken days to pass around it. They paused from time to time to inspect the nearer landing pods, looking hopefully up the darkening sides for hidden openings into the main ship. But there were no openings in the pods or elsewhere. The exploring plant-creatures had retired for the night, locking their doors behind them. The native plants remained somber and silent in their tubs, patient and green, or else closed up like bats, their protective leaves shriveled around them. The jewel-covered ground had ceased to sparkle and by the time it was almost dark they were forced to abandon their search.

They looked toward the black ship and could barely see its dark top against the failing light. But down near the base there seemed to be little twinkling multi-colored lights outlining an entrance. The entrance itself was lit from within and the light flowed dimly down a ramp where they could see the shapes of irregular life-forms standing in a line, some wearing strangely shaped space suits, others naked or nearly so. They were clearly waiting to pass into the doorway one by one.

The men were curious but also cautious, and they returned to their own door while they could still find it, and let themselves into the comforting brightness.

They shed their space suits slowly, unwilling to take the next and obvious step. But it would shortly be time for the nurse to poke her head into the room, ask if they had had a nice walk, and hold out her arms for the baby. In order to avoid such a forced disclosure, Al finally pounded on the door of the Fastar, and when it was opened a crack, yelled for Irma.

"The nurse will come for the baby in a few minutes," she said crossly, appearing at the door. "What do you need me for?" Nonetheless she slid in easily. She wore a white buttoned coat like the rest of the women and her dark brown hair was freshly washed; it bounced up as she dropped the last few feet to the floor and then settled slowly in a fan about her shoulders. She looked remarkably attractive.

Wiener was the first to find his voice. He described their findings in guilty sounding chronological order. Irma gave a sharp cry and dashed behind the partition. The baby's bed was a mass of wrinkled sheets and she scuffled through them as though she expected to find the child hidden in the folds. The others watched in silent commiseration from the edge of the partition.

Suddenly she froze, stared at one spot in the bed, and began to utter a series of yelps which grew quickly into anguished screams.

"What's the matter!" shouted Al, rushing to lean over her shoulder to see what it was. The others crowded behind him; even Harp was interested.

A small pink worm-like object lay on the crumpled sheet where she had disclosed it during her frenzied search. They stared petrified as they slowly realized that it was an infant's finger.

The men joined Irma in her cries of horror as the significance of the severed finger penetrated their shocked minds. Kidnaped! Their anguish brought both Dr. Fish and Miss Squeeze toppling through the hole, and the wails and hair tearings of the newcomers increased the hubbub in the crowded cubicle.

They searched wildly for a ransom note, except for Irma who remained on her knees where she had fallen, staring fixedly at the finger and stuffing wads of the baby's sheet into her mouth in an effort to collect herself.

Dr. Fish was the first to recover. She sent the nurse back to the Fastar to get morphine and a hypodermic. Upon her return the doctor administered injections to Irma, the nurse, Al, and after some consideration, Harp. Wiener was crouched on the floor as far away from the baby's chamber as he could get, holding his head in his hands and trying to think, his hair roughed up as though his scalp were in pain.

Dr. Fish never used sedatives on herself. She looked around to see what needed doing. The most noticeable thing in the cubicle at present, now that Irma was quiet, was the finger. No one had touched it and it rested on the sheet looking very much alive. She glanced about for a suitable container to put it in and found a petrie dish full of metal scraps beside the computer console. She dumped the contents out on the floor, and with a piece of gauze which she had tidily put into her pocket after emptying the syringe, picked up the finger and placed it with some reverence in the dish. There was no blood on it; it seemed to be remarkably clean cut. She looked for a place to put the dish and with unusual sentiment set it carefully on a small shelf beside the crib, where the baby's toys had lain close to her hand: an assortment of rattles, shapes and chewables, made so lovingly for her by her parents and friends. Tears began to well up in Dr. Fish's eyes.

But she did not give way to them. Instead she summoned Wiener to help her force the grumpy and complaining Irma up the hastily assembled steps and through the hole into the Fastar. The nurses's turn came next, then the doctor's. With the help of the reliable Miss Constable the now sleepy women were laid on clean cots and their shoes removed.

MISCHIEF

Wiener and Dr. Fish spent the rest of the day together, not exactly companionably, but at least not quarreling. By an unspoken agreement they avoided the subject of the kidnaping, knowing that they had already said all there was to say. She showed interest in his electrical and mechanical arrangements and in return he submitted to a critical evaluation of the warts on his hands, but declined with restraint her offers to remove them with hypnosis. Afterwards they settled down to read instruction booklets, of which Wiener had a large collection.

She allowed herself to be hoisted back into the Fastar in order to consult with Miss Constable as to the feeding the remaining baby and to check the pulses of the two heavily drugged women, then brought the infant to the port for Wiener to look at. He viewed it carefully; it did not resemble the missing girl, but it did look a bit like his own younger brother whom he had loathed from the day he was born. His brother had grown up to be a flabby singer of sentimental ballads, and Wiener hoped that if the child did prove to be of his getting it would take after Irma rather than his side of the family. Dr. Fish put the baby away, puttered about a bit in the Fastar, then dropped back through the port hole with a freshly heated frozen dinner for two. She sat near Wiener while they ate, read and listened to the snores of Al and Harp.

After endless waiting, the speaker connecting them to the Radial began to hiss and crackle. Next came the welcome gargle of Tak inquiring politely about their health and asking if they had enjoyed their little excursion. He could see them perfectly well through his peep-hole: the unexpected sight of the beautiful Eustacia slumming with the natives, and the two men passed out on the floor, who were now beginning to groan.

The sound of his voice brought hope. But when they had explained the tragic situation to him he only laughed wetly and horribly. The offended Dr. Fish listened to his tasteless mirth with cold detachment.

"Do you not know that the Rda has taken her?" chortled Tak. "It is the only possible explanation. Never will he allow that child to come to harm; you have therefore no reason for alarm." He continued to giggle.

"But that's impossible!" shouted Wiener.

"You merely assume that; you do not know it. You pitiful humans, limited by your miserable two-lobed brains to asking questions one at as time and then answering them with a simple yes or no. You have to build a big messy logical bush to arrive at any conclusion, and it takes all day. Then you invent a computer to do the same thing only faster. Whereas I, with my marvelous multiple cerebral lobes, can consider all possibilities at once! I tell you that the baby is with the Rda."

"But how? Why?"

"Just because you don't know the answer doesn't mean that it's not true," sneered Tak.

Al woke up at the noise and started to swear drowsily. Harp mumbled peevishly without opening his eyes; it sounded like "Water, Water." He began to whimper without making much noise. In contrast the loud speaker began to blare its loudest; Tak had turned it up so as to better make his point.

"Is there not missing a plastic bag?" he roared. Wiener and the Doctor looked around, but the bulkheads were so disheveled by the earlier search that they could not tell if one were missing or not. And when Tak heard about the finger they had found in the child's bed he laughed even more.

"Yes indeed," he advised after his chuckles had stopped shaking the furniture, "Some creature must be holding the child for ransom, for it is the habit on Earth for kidnappers to cut off one of the fingers of the children they steal. It is obviously the only conclusion you could come to as an Earth person. Very well, you are probably right. There is some treasure that you hold here that the kidnapper wants, so he has stolen the baby in order to force you to give it up. Let me see. What can the treasure be? Think, use your lobes. Some valuable instrument, the fruit of some Terrestrial technological advance? Or perhaps a beautiful human female? What can the ransom price be?"

There did not seem to be anything of value that they could exchange for the child. Dr. Fish did have a sizable store of drugs, but it contained nothing unique. Perhaps she had some substance that was rare and priceless in the outer reaches of space. She hastily agreed to supply whatever was demanded from her.

"I, Myself, Tak, will met with these vandals and treat with them and overcome them in argument," announced the Radial generously. He turned down the speaker a little so they could understand him better. "I will bargain with them. I shall emerge from my environment at great inconvenience to myself and enter the hostile atmosphere of this cold, dry planet and endeavor to save the baby." There was a lengthy pause, then his voice came again in an especially choked gurgle.

"Encase the human Harp in a space suit to keep him fresh until the bargaining is over, and put him in the vestibule. I will take him away with me and use him for bait in the preliminary negotiations."

Harp woke up fully at this threat: he cursed in a high voice, jumped to his feet and edged as far away from the others as possible. Dr. Fish began to prepare her syringe while Al and Wiener deployed and began to approach the uncooperative youth from both sides.

"Now no one is going to hurt you," said the Doctor tonelessly, readying the hypodermic.

"Don't you stick them needles in me no more!" yelled Harp, who prepared to go down fighting and to take everyone present with him, including all the breakables in the hated cubicle.

As a preliminary move he snatched at a small control box wired to the wall behind him, tore it from its moorings and hurled it at Wiener.

"No!" shouted Wiener. "No! He's got the hydro's thermostat!" He dodged as it flew by his shoulder and crashed against the wall. "Stop him! Don't let him touch the oscillator!" But it was too late, and the box lay dented on the floor emitting sparks. Then all the lights went out and sputtering stopped.

"Now keep calm, everyone," said Wiener soothingly. "I'll soon have the emergency power cut in." He lit a small flashlight and began to shuffle around in the dark. The loud speaker of the radial was not out of order though, and he could be heard giving advice and encouragement.

"Don't move, anybody," commanded Tak. "Some one could easily be killed with all that loose energy ricocheting about. And Harp, shame on your cowardice! If you come quietly I'll give you a glass of water, a big glass, a very big glass. And a shot of liquor, for I see that the lovely Eustacia has forgotten to give you your afternoon dose."

"If you put on your space suit you will be safe from Dr. Fish and her needle, for the material is so thick that she will not be able to puncture it. Then if you'll come with me you'll never be hurt again, for the vandals will know how to value you. It was you they undoubtedly wanted from the beginning, and they have stolen the baby just to get hold of you. Now after going to all that bother do you think they would want to hurt you, a valuable man of common sense? Of course not. They might even adopt you and you could help them in their exciting raids in outer space." His watery voice was soothing to Harp, for water was what he longed for most of the time. Tak's voice gurgled along something like the mountain stream that flowed over small rocks near Harp's old home in the nature preserve.

"As soon as the lights are functional again, put on your space suit and wait for me in the air lock. Remember, I will have a glass of water for you. If these people try to stop you I will burn them with one of my tentacles which are now protruding through the wall, though you cannot see them in the dark. Remember these people are your enemies; if you stay with them they will only hurt you more and more."

"They have been keeping you prisoner all this time. They may want to prevent you from leaving, but you have protection; the Kidnappers have the baby as a hostage and these enemies of yours will not dare hold you back." His voice became softer and softer. "Now remember, put on your suit as soon as the lights go on and wait for me at the door. They will stare at you and want to stop you, but will not dare. They will not move. You will see." His voice sounded now like a tiny trickle of water passing over a stone or two, as though Harp were lying half asleep next to a mountain stream with his eyes shut.

The lights came back on. As Tak had promised, Al and Dr. Fish were seated on the floor, ignoring Harp except for occasional quick glances. Wiener was putting away some tools in a cabinet, not looking at him at all. Harp crouched down and crawled carefully to where his suit hung slack from its hook on the wall. But no one noticed; they seemed to have gone to sleep, lulled also by Tak's voice. When he was almost dressed and had reached the point where he would need help putting on his helmet, Al spoke softly.

"Good-bye Harp. I'm sorry you're leaving. Can I help you fasten your helmet?" Harp nodded, tears beginning to run down his cheeks. Al had been the only one who was ever kind to him.

"Have a lump of sugar," said Dr. Fish, taking one out of her pocket. She extended it at arm's length, but Harp ignored it. "You'd better not forget this," she said more briskly, and held out a pint bottle which she had drawn out of her pocket along with the sugar.

Harp looked up at the clinking sound, and snatching the bottle with his gloved hand, attempted to unscrew the cap with clumsy fingers. Al did it for him and Harp drank about a quarter of the contents. Then he loosened his neck piece, crammed the bottle down inside his suit and patted the place where it lay to make sure it was secure. He fastened his neck piece again, and accepting the lump of sugar proffered by Al this time, allowed him to place it within the dome of the helmet before it was screwed on, so that it lay a little to one side of his chin where he could capture it with his tongue if he wanted it. All the time tears ran down his cheeks, which could be seen dimly through the helmet's dome. No one looked away.

Finally there was a tap on the air-lock door, which was the signal for Harp to enter the pressure chamber. Al released the catch, the door squeaked open and Harp crawled in with the aid of Al's hand against the small of his back. He received a reassuring pat just before he passed through. Then the door was closed and latched.

"Not a bad little bugger," said Al for his memorial, gazing at the closed door. Then he thought of something and turned abruptly to Dr. Fish. "How long will that pint last him?"

"Around twelve hours, I think. Do you believe Tak can be relied on to return him undamaged if he is not wanted for exchange purposes? I must say I shall find his absence inconvenient to my research plan."

A slight sound from behind the baby's partition disturbed their thoughts. It sounded like a creak from the baby's bed, and was followed by the sound of several small crashes, similar to that made by the baby pulling all her toys off the shelf at once.

They crept around the partition, afraid to believe their ears. The baby was sitting up cheerfully in her bed, batting around her belongings, which now included the petrie dish that had recently been added to her collection by the Doctor. The child was much dirtier than usual, and was powdered with dust which had caked in places into mud. But she smiled and exhibited her front teeth and waved her grubby hands gleefully in greeting.

The doctor was the first to count the baby's fingers. There were five on each hand. She drew this to the attention of the others, and stunned by the illogic of it, they searched the bed and tumbled the baby about in their hunt for the eleventh finger. They examined the floor and all the flat surfaces in the room, for the baby was accustomed to hurl objects a good distance, but the search was fruitless.

It was Al who remembered Harp, who now appeared to have been made into an unnecessary sacrifice. He ran to the door of the pressure chamber and tried the handle. It was no longer locked, which meant that Harp had already passed outside.

"The baby is very dirty, is she not?" remarked a sweet whistling voice. Then the Rda appeared, coiled artistically through the rungs of the baby's bed. This was the first time Dr. Fish had heard his voice or seen him. She jumped with a little squeal and he smiled delightedly and continued his remarks. "Such consternation I have never before had the pleasure of observing in humans. If I had expected it, I would have mentioned that I was planning to take the baby for a little excursion so she could enjoy herself while her elders sought their own amusement on this dark dull planet. Indeed, if I had thought, I would have brought her back earlier, but you know how little time means to me." He shook his head playfully so that his antennae quivered, and the baby snatched at them in delight. She was in an unusually good humor.

"We were gone for so long that she became hungry, something I had not thought of either, for I seldom require nourishment, and when I do I can find it almost anywhere. It was difficult discovering something she was willing to ingest but at last I succeeded."

"What?" asked the Doctor suspiciously.

At that moment the baby made a grab for the Rda with her ten good fingers. They met around his body, and with a sharp unbabylike pull they yanked off a segment of his serpentine form. The break closed instantly and the Rda was once more complete, not at all ruffled by the experience, and the baby had added a segment of the Rda to her pile of toys. It was a slice about four inches thick and two inches in diameter, and had three blue eyes at one end of it, a smiling triangular mouth and three delicate antennae which began to uncurl.

"Then little Hoppy jumped hop! hop! hop! out of his cozy hole," began the segment in a tiny voice. "And the big bad

Bugbear came bump! bump!" There was a pause. "But you shall have no more story until you have had a bath." The mouth pursed disapprovingly shut and the baby began to scream with rage while the humans cringed at the sound.

The baby kicked and squalled but found that she was not getting sufficient reaction to her ploy. In her fury she started tearing at her fingers, pulling three of them off one hand and casting them in the direction of the stunned onlookers.

"Now stop that!" shrilled the Rda. He appealed to the humans. "You'll have to help me pick them up and put them back on. That is one thing I am not good at, and she knows it! She usually puts her hands back together by herself, but when she's cross you can't do a thing with her."

He flailed around inefficiently on the floor trying to sweep the three fingers into a pile. But Eustacia, undeterred by the flying body parts because of her medical experience, had snatched them up and was busy fitting them back on the little hand. It was difficult at first to get the right finger not only in the right place but with the fingernail the right way up. Once fitted on correctly, with no seam showing, in the same way that the Rda himself came apart and went back together, the result was satisfying but also quite sickening, as the doctor began to understand the biological implications of the child's abnormal proclivities.

The men, however, did not have not her experience and self-control; they raced for the toilet, and with Al getting there first, Wiener had to be content with the sink. Dr. Fish, the first part of her mission completed, shouted for Miss Constable. Then she picked the baby up in her sheet like a bundle of washing, and without getting her hands or her white coat dirty, carried the unsanitary pile to the door of the Fastar and handed it up to the waiting nurse.

"Are the mother and Miss Squieze conscious?"

"No, Doctor. They started to wake up, but were so restless that I gave them another dose."

"Excellent. Please be advised, Miss Constable, that the fingers and probably the toes of this child have become extremely brittle. Please try to prevent her from playing with them. When I return I will tape them securely."

"Now, then," she turned and faced the Rda, who was of two minds whether or not he wished to remain and listen to what he knew was coming. "I understand the situation exactly. These two simple men may have been fooled, but I am a woman and conversant besides with the laws of genetics. What I wonder is, how did you manage to fool the mother?" Her beautiful face became that of an enraged Samurai prepared to avenge his family. "And just what responsibility do you intend to take for the support and upbringing of your daughter?" The Rda disappeared in the blink of an eye.

"Bravo!" came a watery shout from Tak's intercom. He of course had been listening and enjoying it all. "The Rda goes where he pleases, when he pleases. Do not be too sure of your genetics; he is capable of having added selected material to the embryo. In other respects the child may be the normal product of a human union. I suggest further testing before giving way to violence."

"You knew about this all along!"

"Certainly. The Rda is well known for this kind of behavior. After all, there are no female Rdas; he is the only one. This is his method of propagation. Incidentally, if he can prove that he is at least 50% the parent, under Universal Law he can demand custody of the child."

With a stream of denunciations, Dr. Fish summoned the men to help her and climbed awkwardly up the tottering steps into the Fastar. Once inside, she slammed the door.

TAK AT HOME

Harp had no illusions about the kindness of extraterrestrials toward humans. The Rda, for one, had never seemed to notice him, and the Radial, represented in Harp's imagination as a loud-voiced card playing set of tentacles, had not noticed him either, except on that first day when he had recommended that Harp be given a drink of water when he was thirsty. So when Tak had offered him as a fair exchange for the baby he had not felt it as a betrayal, merely as an expected cruelty.

Harp's faith in the kindness of his fellow humans had also never been strong and had daily grown weaker. The original horror of his capture and sacrifice on the Altar of Science had already sunk into his heart and had been dismissed into his deepest and almost forgotten memories, where it mingled with those acquired in childhood as the casually raised son of alcohol befuddled parents. He had not even bothered to appeal to the better natures of his fellow humans, for he knew that he was only an experimental animal. Al, the kindest one, had treated him like a stray dog and had good naturedly not kicked him, but that was about as far as it had gone. And the prince, who had thoughtlessly treated him more as an equal, had abandoned him without a thought. As Harp felt himself pushed through the door into the pressure chamber only one ray of hope remained.

He repressed it, as was his habit, but it still glowed dimly. It was based on logic, not trust. The Radial was a water-loving creature, for he lived in steam, which was a form of water. He had just promised Harp a glass of the same if he would come quietly. He seemed likely to keep this particular small promise, and if he told the truth about one thing he might be reliable in others, even the promise that the Vandals would not hurt him. Therefor he deduced, in an unprecedented burst of logic brought on by his awareness of danger and the consequent sharpening of his wits, that he would soon be able to slake his thirst by gulping water instead of soaking it slowly and inadequately through a tube into his veins. Also he might be able to look forward to what remained of his short life without being an experiment, though that hope remained vague in the timid recesses of his mind.

It was with reveries of this sort that he squeezed through the aperture into the pressure chamber and heard the door clang shut behind him. He had visualized the Radial as a sort of octopus, as pictured in his school books, but nervously dismissed the sneaking idea that it might be man-eating.

The air warmed rapidly around him; he could feel it through his space suit. He pulled at the handle of the outside door and found himself looking into a plastic tunnel, not large enough to stand up in, which curved away to the left. Nothing better offering, he crawled down it for ten feet or so and found himself looking into a brightly lit circular room about sixty feet across which was empty except for a dripping water tap and a foot of water on the floor.

It looked like water anyway. He ventured one space suited hand into it. It felt like water, and rather hot, too. Chiefly because he was tired of crouching in the tunnel, he squeezed through into the room and stood up. The door shut automatically behind him.

The water around his feet was definitely too hot, though the insulation in his suit prevented them from becoming parboiled. However, his rapidly heating legs made the rest of his body sweaty and made him dizzy, so he undid his gloves, dropped them in the water, and with his fingers free unfastened the screws of his helmet and flipped it back on its hinge so it hung down behind him. But the steaming air entering his lungs made him feel even fainter and he suddenly sat down in the hot water and passed out.

When Harp awoke he was shivering with cold: there must have been some transitional events, but he was too confused to figure them out. He knew that his space suit was gone, that his clothes were soaking wet and that he was lying half in and half out of a large pile of crushed ice. It felt terrible, almost burning, and he struggled his way clear and stood up in a small room that was dimly lit and lined with frost-encrusted pipes. The floor was littered with irregular piles of crushed ice; the pieces skittered under his feet, which were bare, and he found it difficult to walk. He stumbled over to some large metal canisters which stood half buried in the ice. One was tipped on its side and seemed to be filled with frozen spinach. It was a relief to see something that he recognized: chopped hydroponics. A plastic bag full of some live thing was also lying on the ice. It heaved softly.

He did not have time to examine his surroundings; the most important task was to escape before he froze. He searched for a door but could not find it. One wall was devoid of pipes; it was perfectly smooth, not even disfigured by lumps of adhering ice. He started kicking frantically at the wall, sobbing to himself between shudders as he hurt his already painful feet.

To his surprise and relief the whole wall gave way. It was hinged at the bottom and fell outward with a crash. It stopped falling when it reached the level of the floor, and he stumbled out onto the platform it created into a delicious rush of warm air. He thought of nothing else but to open his arms and breathe the hot air gratefully until the frost burns receded and he stopped shivering.

He was standing on a shelf that extended about eight feet into a large booming chamber, which he recognized as the watery room he had encountered at the end of the tunnel. Small clouds and wisps of steam floated before his eyes, obscuring his view of the farther walls. Looking down he noticed that the water on the floor was much deeper now; his shelf stood only a few feet above the surface. A large gray shapeless mass about ten feet across floated in it, disappearing and reappearing. It looked like a gigantic floor-mop, much like the one his mother had sloshed up and down in a pail of water when he was a child. But this one was alive, its long yarn-like tentacles writhing and crawling in a complicated pattern.

But before he could come to further conclusions he had to get out of the heat. He backed away from the edge of the platform until he stood just inside the cold room among the now melting piles of ice. The frigid water trickled by his feet on its way to join the lake in the room below. With cold behind and heat in front he found his situation bearable, but moved forwards and backwards until he found the best combination and pronounced himself comfortable. He looked around for something to sit on, rejected the squirming object in the plastic bag, and settled for an upturned canister.

Only then did he notice that the symbol of his servitude, the feeding tube, was missing from the back of his hand. There were red weals that felt like blisters around the wound and he felt other painful spots on his arms and ankles and neck.

He suddenly remembered his bottle of alcohol and looked wildly around for it. He found his shoes partly buried in a pile of ice, retrieved them and prepared to put the stiff things back on his feet as the first move in navigating the sharp ice chips in his hunt for the lost bottle. But he desisted when he discovered the object of his search frozen into one shoe. He could not get it out, but it was head up and he was able to unscrew the cap and drink about half of what was left. He tucked the shoe with the nearly empty bottle inside his coverall to warm them; they were horribly cold and he leaned forward so they wouldn't press too much against his chest. In the other shoe he found a small plastic packet. It proved to contain some lumpy bits of sugar. He remembered it now. It must have been the Radial who had packaged it to keep it from dissolving in the damp. Harp felt a small surge of gratitude as he realized that the Radial had also preserved him, like the sugar, from the boiling steam bath by packing both in ice. He resolved to save the sugar until he really needed it; the packet and contents went into his wet pocket.

The drink had dispelled most of his worries. He looked again over the platform; it was just as well he was no longer standing in the ice room, for as soon as he stepped over the big hinge which served as a threshold a shower of fresh ice chips exploded from the ceiling and crashed onto the floor. Some of the flying chips struck him as they bounced and they felt soothing to his already heating skin.

A huge head, about four feet across, rose slowly out of the water. He knew it was a head from its two bulbous eyes and sharp beak.

"Greetings," said Tak, for of course it was he. "I hope you will kindly accept my apologies for overlooking your temperature requirements on your arrival. I believe I almost lost you. I am also afraid I burnt you, though not seriously, while carrying you to my refrigerator for revival. I suggest you do not stray far from it if you value your health." Harp looked at the weals on his skin and realized how hot the Radial must be.

"No more intra-venous feeding for you, my little friend. You can now eat delicious seaweed, boiled, and drink water to your heart's content. I have saved you from your fellow savages' death rites and will shortly return you to your natural habitat on Earth, or failing that, to one that suits you better. I consider it a crime to attempt adaptation of a species; the demented members of RES have overstepped themselves again and will have to be taught a lesson. You will be used as an example of this crime. That is why I have been kind to you; I have no particular interest in you as an individual specimen. What do you think of that?"

"What about my whiskey?" whined Harp. "How about the Vandals? They won't hurt me?"

"There are no Vandals, Human. The Universe has been cleansed of crime once and for all by the Aubudon Society. No kidnappers. Your stupid companions did not believe me when I told them the truth, that the baby had merely been borrowed by the Rda. So I made a little amusement for myself by persuading them to believe the ridiculous rather than the obvious, which is a common failing in your species."

"What about my whiskey? I've got to have whiskey. I'll die without it!" urged Harp.

"Ah yes, your dietary requirements. Unwholesome of course. I am tempted to try sudden withdrawal. However, I will see what I can do."

"I've got to have it." Harp's voice rose. He was aware that it was unwise to try temper, considering his wholly dependent position, but the prize was worth the risk.

"Quiet!" commanded Tak. "I am putting my minds to your problem." He sank out of sight with a heavy gasp, but reappeared almost immediately.

"What is the chemical formula for your toxic drink?"

"What?" asked Harp. "Oh, it's made from rye or wheat mash. You let the mash ferment, then heat it and cool it through coils. It's called distilling."

The Radial sank again in thought. When he rose he said, "Give me a sample. I will analyze it by the taste."

"I haven't any more," said Harp hurriedly.

"Nonsense, give it to me." A tentacle extended itself over the ledge and began to grope sightlessly in his direction.

"Wait a minute!" shouted Harp. He handed his precious bottle over to the tentacle, which coiled carefully around it. The bottle disappeared over the edge. It was returned almost immediately, with, to be fair, only a very little of the life-giving liquid missing. Harp seized it, cautious not to burn his fingers on the hot meal cap, opened it with the aid of his coverall pocket and took a good swig. Then he sat down on a pile of ice to restore his equilibrium. But curiosity overcoming him, he approached the edge of the platform again.

"Did you like it?" he asked Tak "It's a good brand."

"Not bad. Interesting sugar possibilities. Quiet, now. I'm thinking." He thought for a few moments. "Ah, I have it. It will be easy to synthesize. Of course I shall have to borrow supplies from your neighbors, but that is only a small matter of drilling holes into their apartments without their being the wiser. Perhaps I shall ask the Rda to help me with this. Water weed will make an

84

excellent base to begin with. This will probably turn out to be an amusing project. Now go back into the refrigerator, close the door and get some sleep."

"No, no!" cried Harp. "Not in there. I'll freeze."

"You will? Then I have not perfectly regulated your environment for your comfort. Never mind. As we get better acquainted your living conditions will be more nearly approach the optimal. It is a matter of principle to me to make your environment adapt to you, rather than have you adapt to your environment as that trouble-making Dr. Fish would do. I am one of the officials of the Society for the Maintenance of Endangered Species, the MES; we do not agree with the methods of the Society for the Relocation of Endangered Species, in which Dr. Fish is a very minor functionary. Here on the Imbalancia, where I may say without pride that I am a major functionary, as the only one who thoroughly understands its navigational principals, the RES will be unable to do its dirty work without protective guidelines, whatever damage it may perpetrate on unobserved worlds. Do you understand?"

"Oh yes, thank you Sir. I am deeply grateful. If I might have something to eat? Or a glass to drink out of?"

"All in good time. But you will never appreciate my approach to the perfect environment for you with your distressingly limited stochastic understanding. What a pity. I would have enjoyed an intelligent companion. However, I will endure you for the principle of the thing. In the meantime have some boiled water-weed." He sank out of sight.

It would take too long to describe Harp's efforts to boil some of the water-weed in a canister, or to praise fully enough his diligence in achieving that goal. Most of his under clothing was sacrificed in order to make rope to lower a partly filled canister into the steamy water below. He cooked by the sweat of his brow as he leaned over the infernal double-boiler. At last the mess was cooked, hauled in, cooled with ice and eaten. And even then he could force down but little, for he had made do for such a long time with scraps from the delegates' table, snacks from the generous prince, and plenty of sugar water and alcohol delivered antiseptically through his veins.

He lay back replete against the plastic bag which proved to be warm and soft like a pillow. Its occasional squirming did not bother him. He washed down his watery meal with all but a half inch of the remaining whiskey.

He slept for many hours. He knew this because when he awoke he had a craving for the last mouthfuls. He sadly finished them except for a few drops. Then he realized that he was actually hungry for more of the disgusting looking boiled water-weed. He walked over to the canister which contained the remains of his previous meal. He had left it near the middle of the ledge instead of on ice, and it was smelly and sour to the taste. Nevertheless he scooped out a handful of the soggy mess and stuffed it into his mouth. To his surprise he felt better immediately.

He noticed an increase in the heat coming from the indoor lake and turning found Tak's head nearby and on a level with his own body. The head was hooked comfortably onto the ledge by its curved beak, which served for a nose or a mouth, and one of its serious gray eyes gazed roundly at him. He edged back toward the ice box to remove himself from both the gaze and the heat. The Radial hitched himself onto the ledge more firmly with two tentacles and disengaged his beak so he could talk. His voice was clearer than it had been over the loud speaker, but there was still a gurgle to confuse the ear. Harp accounted for this strange sound by deciding that Tak's lungs were half-full of water.

"Your toxic drink is coming along nicely. Within one of your earth hours the first lot should be distilled. Fermentation was very fast. I mixed some of my most volatile water weed with hydroponics grown by your earth men, which I drained quietly from their tank, and added a yeast of such virulence that I usually keep it frozen. Some of my own plumbing with the water removed served as a fermenting and boiling vat. For cooling I surreptitiously utilized some of the lighting tubes of my neighbor the Triffid, who has more light than even he, with his photon craving, could ever need. He is super-cautious and has an excess of everything, but is not one from whom you can ask favors. His cool atmosphere is swifter for distillation than my own cozy home. The heated brew has yielded a few drops already and I have sampled them. It is indeed a delicious concoction; I wonder that my people on Vpor have not conducted this experiment before, though perhaps the need to keep the distillation process cool would prohibit it. Give me the remainder of the liquid in your bottle. I will test it against the new lot and compare them with the aid of my discriminating palate."

Without asking permission he snaked a tentacle out and grasped Harp's bottle, which was standing unguarded nearby. In any case Harp would not have disputed ownership with one of the alien's blistering limbs. Tak sucked up the last drops before the owner's woeful eyes.

"Almost identical, except for the superior delicacy of my mixture. Mine is also a little raw; perhaps if it is allowed to settle for a short time. Soon there will be several canisters full of the drink, and this raises a problem: unfortunately my distilling apparatus is so large that I am forced to make a great amount or none at all. By tomorrow there will be enough of the liquid to cover the floor of my home several tentacles deep."

"Don't you worry about that," said Harp heartily, beginning to lick his lips.

"Don't be ridiculous" said Tak. "The excess will not spoil and there should be enough for several of your lifetimes, but my canister supply is limited and I cannot afford to tie up so many for such a long period. I can eject the excess secretly onto the planet below, where it may do some damage, or give it away to curious neighbors, or try to burn it as fuel or even drink it myself. But I cannot think of anything else as a possibility, which is odd for a Radial of my mental capacity."

"Why not sell it?"

"To whom? Your fellow humans? Barter it, you mean? But surely they have no room in their cubicle for anything more, even though I have half emptied their hydroponics tank. Furthermore I have not observed in any one of the humans a desire for this stuff at all comparable to yours.

"As to selling the fluid to other delegates in the Assembly: To my certain knowledge none of them metabolize this sort of thing except the Fix from Enulaf, for that planet has an alcohol dissolved lithosphere. But the Fix already have their own supply, and as they are extremely small their entire ration would fit easily into your little bottle. Also I have not seen them or their cubicle for many years; it is so tiny that it probably has become corroded into a small cranny of the Imbalancia. They are no larger than your smallest earth bacteria, and are not much sought out because they tend to burrow their crustacean-like claws into whatever living substance they can find, and settle inside to create their own alcohol there. I had thought of catching a few and applying them to your blood stream, but no, that would have been too experimental for a Radial of my principles. Tempting, of course. But also I could not find them; that must be considered, too."

Harp paid little attention to what the Radial was saying; the memory of his bottle disappearing over the ledge remained foremost in his mind.

"You may not realize it," he said indignantly, "but if I have to wait more than an hour for a drink I am liable to die. I am sure it has been at least that long by now. As a matter of fact, I am beginning to choke." Here he clutched his neck with one hand and choked himself a little. "For God's sake," he gurgled, "I can't wait much longer."

Alarmed, the Radial sank under the water. Harp let go of his throat and looked earnestly at his hands; they were not yet beginning to shake. Instead he felt hungry, which was an unaccustomed sensation, so he ate more of the nauseating green mush. He resolved to cook the next meal more efficiently.

The Radial returned and raised himself onto the platform.

"The distillation process is so slow," he mourned. "Only a few drops have emerged since I last looked. It was not even worth bringing, so I drank it myself. And now I am tired; my eyes are strained with all the work I have been doing for your benefit. I will go to sleep." He began to submerge slowly back into the water.

Harp was horrified. "Not yet!" he shouted. "You can't leave me like this!" But the Radial closed his eyes and continued to sink. Harp seized the only thing at hand, a chunk of ice, and hurled it at the alien. At the first touch of the burning ice the Radial cried out in pain and submerged until only one eye remained above the water and glared at Harp. Then Tak raised his beak above the surface the better to shout.

"What are you doing, you nasty little cold Earth creature? How do you dare? Have you gone mad?"

"Yes, I have gone mad!" answered Harp obligingly. "Mad with the need for alcohol. We Earth creatures sometimes slash, main and tear with unnatural strength if we are deprived of our addictive substances." He delivered a series of inaccurate Karate chops and kicks at the air, almost losing his balance.

"I had no idea" said Tak reproachfully. "Wait and I'll bring you some at once. I can't let a fellow creature suffer."

True to his promise the Radial returned almost immediately with Harp's bottle filled with steaming liquid. Harp poured a small amount into the cap, added a sliver of ice and sampled it. It was fiercely burning, very satisfying, and had no taste to speak of.

Two or three capfulls later he congratulated Tak. "It's the real stuff all right. I couldn't do better myself. But it needs a bit of flavor to pep it up."

"I have just the thing!" roared Tak genially, and dove from view. He returned with a dripping bunch of leaves clutched in one tentacle and thumped them onto the ledge at Harp's feet.

"There you are, Friend," he howled in a voice of tearful exaltation. "The flower of Vpor, the tender Lauchet; sought in vain throughout the Universe as the ultimate panacea, its whereabouts known only to a few of the chosen! Dip it in your drink, taste it and weep!"

Harp did as he was told. He bruised an already wet leaf, dropped it into the cap with ice, added alcohol and tried it. It did do something, but not much.

"Delicious," roared Tak, roused from his earlier

somnolence. "And now, my little Friend, we will put on our space suits and visit the smugglers in their Black Ship, drink the fiery liquid with them, strike an advantageous bargain, and see what they have brought me in the way of amusing art films. Get dressed, hurry!" Harp's space suit, soaking wet, flew through the steamy air and landed with a squelch on the ledge beside him. He looked over the edge to protest but Tak had already disappeared.

SMUGGLERS DEN

It took quite some time for Harp to get into his space suit because it was soggy and resisted his bodily movements. His clothes had started to dry a little and he was grieved to get them wet again, but he was really quite afraid of Tak and anxious to remain on his good side. The gloves were missing but there were straps that he could tighten around his wrists. He stowed his bottle carefully next to his heart and swallowed a quick handful of hydroponics. Then he sat down to wait, his helmet hanging down his back by its hinge. He would have gone to sleep if he had not been so uncomfortable, for Tak was gone a long time.

He suddenly noticed, approaching through the fog and steam, a small red inflated raft curled up around the edges so that it appeared to be a kind of boat. The Radial was not in sight, but Harp soon discerned him beneath the raft helping it along. Tak flipped it awkwardly into the ledge while Harp dodged out of its way, knowing it would be hot, then kicked it onto the ice to cool. Tak moved clumsily, for his space suit had no more than a dozen arms and the numerous other tentacles crammed inside his suit got in each other's way. He seemed to be as uncomfortable as Harp, who wondered why he had chosen to go to such lengths just to visit some neighbors.

The Radial had not yet pulled the suit's huge plastic dome over his head so that Harp jumped when he shouted. "Don't let that thing touch my Anebit! It's delicate!"

"What Anebit?" asked Harp, confused.

"That Anebit right next to your feet. It's far more precious to me than you are, so watch it!"

Harp looked down, but there was nothing evident except the plastic bag which contained the red, warm, soft thing he had used as a pillow while sleeping. He had thought it was something Tak was saving for his dinner, some poor living creature that he was refrigerating to keep fresh, like Harp himself. Harp had assumed that the Radial intended to boil it when he was ready to eat it, as people on earth did with clams. Right now it was wiggling excitedly.

Tak poked it lightly with a tentacle and then gave it little gentle rubs. "It likes to be tickled. I would keep it in my pocket at all times were I not afraid that it would wear out too fast from the heat. I promised my uncle, who gave it to me long ago, that I would keep it oiled and give it long cool rests. It's a kind of computer and is my most precious possession. Don't touch it. I don't want it to clutter up its exclusive memory with thoughts of you. Aren't you precious, my little precious?" He tickled it some more. "Without it I wouldn't be able to hold my important position as the Imbalancia's navigator because for the past thousand or so of your earth years I have become progressively more senile. I can still do almost all possible calculations, but my memory is terrible; it always was and is now getting worse. If the Anebit were alive and not just a computer it would be my best friend."

The Radial became more businesslike. "Come, Harp, the boat's cool enough now for you to handle it. I acquired it for you with the greatest effort and expense. I hope you are grateful. I don't want you to get your feet wet again, as it causes no end of trouble. It will also double as a bed. I've gone to such extremes to make you comfortable!"

Tak pulled his enormous headpiece shut and fastened it. Harp noticed that the tips of some of the space suit's arms were tied in knots. It looked like a very old suit. He fastened his own helmet, lowered the raft into the steaming water and climbed gingerly aboard while the Radial held it steady. There was a little red paddle in the boat and he paddled swiftly to the door of the pressure chamber, with Tak shoving from behind.

Harp climbed out of the boat and shut himself into the chamber as Tak had instructed him. There was no longer a plastic tunnel leading to the earth capsule; it had been replaced by a roomy air-lock with doors on all four sides. After a short wait the outside door clinked open and he slid down a chute onto the dark planet. It was comforting to see that the sky was full of stars. The sight made him feel homesick. He could see in his mind's eye the little trickling brook that tumbled through the woods near his mountain home. Tears streamed down his cheeks but the helmet prevented him from wiping them away. When he returned to the present he was fully aware of his loneliness and helplessness. One hand rested on a metal ring at the end of the chute and it was this alone that kept him from complete disorientation.

After what seemed like an endless wait the door flew open again, light streamed out and Tak slid down emitting heat and comfort. With a beckoning gesture from one of his tentacles, and using some of the others for locomotion, Tak set out with Harp close behind. The translucent chute gave off a glow that made a path of light for them to follow.

When they reached the end of the illuminated area the tip of one of Tak's tentacles began to shine. Harp saw that it ended in a sort of flashlight attachment. He noticed that several other arms also ended in mechanical contrivances, whose uses he could not guess, though one appeared in the dim light to be a sort of monkey wrench and he could swear that another was a can opener. However there was no way to ask.

Gradually Tak ended his forward motion and pointed his light upward. Above their heads was a black metal surface, studded with rivets, somewhat dented and streaked with rust. The Radial started to flail another of his tentacles, which ended in a black metal ball about two inches across. After a few swings the ball struck the metal surface above with a loud jarring clang.

They waited for a minute or two. Then Tak began to show signs of impatience, swaying his limbs and moving his bulk back and forth. He swung the armed tentacle again and it struck the metal surface with an even louder report.

Almost immediately there was an answering screeching and clanging in the black ceiling above them. A huge trap door slid open, a powerful searchlight shone out and a rusted gangplank began a leisurely and complaining descent. Tak flopped himself onto it when it was only half-way down and swarmed effortlessly up and in through the dark opening at the top. Then the gangplank hit the ground and stood shivering before Harp.

He felt very tired, unwilling to make the effort to climb. All around him was hostile darkness; his suit smelled of burnt plastic and sweat. Before him lay yet another space ship, one in which Tak expected to feel at home, judging from the enthusiasm with which he had mounted the gangplank. That meant it was probably full of hot water and steam. Harp felt faint at the thought of it; he was already beginning to perspire. So he sat down and began to fumble at his headpiece so he could open his suit and get at his bottle. He figured that if he held his breath he would be able to extricate the bottle, take a drink, put it back and even fasten his helmet again before losing consciousness.

"Hey!" a voice from a loudspeaker blared with such volume that he could hear it distinctly through his helmet. "Hurry up, we haven't got all night! Climb the gangplank, asshole!"

Galvanized by the sound of human speech, Harp staggered to his feet, climbed onto the gangplank and clung to the railing with both hands. Fortunately he did not change his mind and try to sit down again, for the gangplank retracted at once, snatching him noisily into the air. Before he could gather his senses he had been hauled inside the belly of the ship and the door had screeched shut behind him.

People from Earth, he thought. Real people. A great weight lifted from his chest, a load that had accumulated so gradually that he had not been consciously aware of it until that moment. He felt that he was at last among friends when he heard the harsh, uncultivated voice of the man who had shouted at him. After his experience as an experimental animal in the hands of Dr. Fish he had learned to suspect the motives of those who spoke in cultured, smooth tones. "Climb the gangplank, asshole" rang sweet and friendly in his ears.

He tried to look around but the air lock was dark. So he waited, still clinging to the foot of the gangplank like a child waiting to be lifted off a trapeze. Before too long a door squealed open and he looked through it into a large untidy room full of bales coming apart, shabby armchairs, the remains of meals and general clutter. He stepped over the high sill. Immediately fingers began to undo his helmet; it was tilted back on its hinges, and wonder of wonders, he smelled tobacco smoke.

"Jesus, hurry,' said a gravelly voice. "Get out that bottle. We've been waiting a couple of months now for a drink. Hurry!" The same hands helped strip down his space suit, another pair of arms started pulling at his feet and he sagged between them.

He found himself lying naked on the floor, for his clothing had stuck so wetly to the suit that they had come off together. But he was glad enough to be free of it. He looked cautiously up at his captors or perhaps rescuers, two brawny men clad in new black coveralls, their faces obscured with hair. They were finishing his bottle of water-weed gin as rapidly as possible, passing it back and forth between them.

"Hey, wait a minute, that's mine!" he shouted, rising suddenly to his feet and grabbing at the nearly empty bottle. They looked at him as though he were a ghost and handed him the bottle immediately. He renewed his nerves with a series of gulps until the flask was empty.

"Look at that," said one of the men, whose hair was dark red and curly. He had bright blue eyes, a round nose and a not unpleasant manner. "That boy thirsts. Just as well there's plenty more in old Taken's larder. I'd hate to have the responsibility of him when he's dry."

The other man, who was thinner and darker in hue, hair and temperament, jerked open a port in the wall. "Hey," he yelled, revealing himself as the owner of the gravelly voice, "Got any more liquor samples in there?" Little puffs of steam escaped from the port, familiar sounds boomed out and a tentacle proffered a sort of milk can, which the dark man seized but quickly dropped when it burnt his hands.

"What are you doing in that hole?" asked Harp nervously.

"Mind your own business!" was the terse reply, and the port cover was slammed shut from within.

"Why do you keep him in there?" he asked while the men hunted up clean glasses and ice cubes.

"We're fuckin' well not going to keep him in here with us!" said the dark headed man. "Him and the rest of our clientele, dirty minded freaks. You haven't been away from earth long, have you. Some of them smell, some of them make you sick to look at, not one of them can sit around and pass the time of day in a reasonable manner; they've always got to be boasting about the superiority of their way of life on some godforsaken planet, one hundred feet deep in ammonia, most likely. We keep old Taken in the hot water tank. See those ports? The cold water tank is next door. After that comes ammonia, then hydrogen, then methane, and last sulfur. That takes care of most of them. We can't suit everybody. The tanks are all connected to the pressure chamber you came through. Did you notice the smell?"

"I had my helmet on."

"Well, the Gooks sit in their nice private tanks and we show them pictures on TV screens set into the ceilings where they can't get at them....Jesus, what bad taste they've got."

The other man handed Harp a towel and a clean bright red coverall. "Put it on; it's a Small. Get those pitiful bones out of sight." Harp climbed gratefully into the suit, not only happy to be dry and clothed but delighted to wear something more colorful than medicinal white or the Nature Preserve's dark green.

"It's one of his fuckin' Holy Highness's suits. We weren't sure of the size so we brought some of each. You'll not be able to wear it on Earth or they'll put you in jail, but up here they're so stupid they don't know the difference."

"Holy Highness?"

"Don't tell me you haven't met darlin' Prince Robert the Bruce! You were holed up with him for months. He was the first one to escape from the Earth capsule and has been whooping it up all over the Imbalancia ever since, running up a big bill. Of course he's good for it, but he doesn't like living here and I don't blame him. As soon as he can get that good looking nurse out of there and away from that Cold Fish, as he calls her, we'll be taking him back to Earth when we head home with our load of gold. We've got almost all we can carry now."

There was a loud banging on the bottom of the ship; it made their feet tingle.

"Another one!" The dark haired man looked through a kind of peephole, swore, and left to admit a new customer.

"What kind of movies do you show them?"

"Sex clips, mostly. Sometimes they want the new films from their own planets, but it takes time to get them and they're expensive. We can film most of the sex clips right here on the ship in no time."

"You make porno movies?"

"We're artists. We make art films," said the red-headed man smoothly. "For all tastes. Don't knock it; it takes a bit of imagination, I can tell you, to devise something that will thrill a sentient block of iron."

"How can you thrill a block of iron?"

"Threaten to spray it with water, for one thing. We found out that if you show them a bunch of water drops they make a squealing noise. Never could communicate with them so can't tell you how they reproduce. Maybe they don't."

"How does Tak get his kicks?" asked Harp interestedly.

"That's easy. Everything on Vpor screws all the time with practically everything else. Non-specific they call it. We just show him anything that looks as though it comes from his home town. He's practically stuck on sponges. We've got a cold water sponge from Loofar that poses for favors received."

"What favors?"

"Never mind. We're in a confidential semi-medical position here and don't tell all we know, not by half," said the red-head. "It's a good business but we don't see much cash; barter is what we do. We buy cheap common trash on one planet and sell it dear on another, and pick up junk of a little more value to add to our stock. The illegal stuff brings the best prices, but it's dangerous. Tricky new computers, ray guns and that sort. We carry mail, too, and passengers who want to travel without fan-fare. The Imbalancia is the best porno market anywhere in the Universe. We went into film production at once when we heard they were in the neighborhood, then flew over and joined them here. We sell films and the delegates pay for them by posing for new films. They're all publicity-mad. Then maybe we'll go back to their home planets and sell the movies to the media, but it all goes in overhead. My God, water-weed gin!"

The door squealed open and the dark-haired man climbed in, followed by another man in a space suit with the helmet laid back. It was the prince! Harp jumped up to help him disrobe and the two red-clad companions embraced each other.

"Isn't that sweet," jeered the dark-haired pirate. "Just like the Bobsey twins." The red-head poured drinks all around.

"Dirty Saki," said the dark one, gulping his distastefully. "Fourteen years and all we have to show for it is this low grade stuff and a beat-up ship. You said we would have a fleet in three years."

"You can't win 'em all," said the red-head automatically. "One thing though, you don't get much company. There are plenty of humans scattered around the Imbalancia but we can't visit them because we're outlaws. Only a few radicals come to see us for cigarettes, booze, drugs or just to talk."

But Harp and the prince were busily engaged in bringing each other up to date. Harp's story was soon told, and the prince laughed heartily over the way Tak had bamboozled the delegates and rescued him from Dr. Fish. But the prince was not altogether pleased that Harp was wearing the Imperial red.

"Why don't you fellows run his wet clothes and space suit through the dryer so he can change. It'll spoil the space suit but he won't need it in this atmosphere. He can wear it and it will still look like a space suit. He doesn't even need the helmet to show he's from the Imbalancia."

"What do you mean? I'll die if I go outside without my suit!"

"Haven't you caught on yet? This planet has a good oxygen atmosphere, though it's a little deficient in gravity. Didn't you see the plants growing? That means oxygen. Don't you know anything?"

"I didn't get very far in school, only to the third grade."

"I don't suppose that really matters," said the prince encouragingly. "We only wear the space suits to show the Walking Plants and Cocci-type Hoppers that we are an already known species. Otherwise they would snatch us up and put us in cages, for they have been instructed to collect two of everything they find if they have never seen it before, and they have remarkably short memories. They operate under the Society for the Collection of Endangered Species, the CES, and those of us unlucky enough to be caught will be placed in the Zoo's permanent collection as new delegates, no matter how we argue. And you can't argue with a plant."

"You know what," said Harp. "I'd really like to go back to Earth."

"I'll be returning myself as soon as I can figure out a way to sneak Miss Squeeze away from Dr. Fish; I am in love with her and she with me. I have decided to marry her and make her a princess. She won't mind. And after she finds out how terrible it is to be a princess, it will be too late, I'll have her!"

"I thought you were never going back until you had found a way to heat the swimming pool."

"I've found a way. I haven't been wandering around in the Imbalancia all this time just to see the sights. It's only necessary to heat a narrow strip ten inches deep down the center of the pool with twin laser beams, dive shallowly, and immediately after leaving the pool, mix the heated water with the cold, using paddles in order to avoid evaporation. We'll lose about a pint a day, but that can be compensated for by replacing the old toilets in the palace with new ones designed to save water. We might even have a net gain in the end!

"It's quite easy to travel around the Imbalancia, for the ship is designed to provide travel routes by arranging similar environments in sequence with doors between them. I've met a good many strange fellows and learned a lot from them, both scientific and political. They were most cooperative when they learned I was a prince. Most of them can speak Esperanto, and some of them Bostonian, for of course that was the original spiritual home of the Aubudon Society. That's one of the first things I intend to take care of when I get back to earth. I'm sick of the way they keep revising the history books for political reasons.

"I also ran into quite a few humans. They looked a little guilty when they saw me, since a number of them are probably spies. I prefer the company of Pat and Rodrigo here. Also, they are my only source for candy bars; there weren't any on the Imbalancia except for those locked up in Dr. Fish's larder. Pat, get me a Hershey bar."

Pat not only got the prince a Hershey bar but gave one to Harp as well and put the latter's wet clothes into the drier. They drank their gin and settled down for a comfortable conversation.

Pat ruminated, "You're a kind of outlaw, Harp, at least a fugitive. Care to join us?"

"I don't expect you'll be very useful," said Rodrigo morosely. "But we can offer you booze when we have it, long cruises and plenty of cosmic radiation if that's your bag. And boredom. We've been marooned on this speckled plant-haven for a week now. Can't get off. All traffic is frozen because of an Elf-star in the neighborhood. The Imbalancia's stuck here just like us, scared to death; they don't dare move, don't dare breathe for fear the Elf-star'll hear them"

"What's an Elf-star?" Neither the prince nor Harp knew.

"You haven't been out of your cradles very long, have you," sneered Rodrigo. "An Elf-star is a little thing no bigger than the palm of your hand. It has five points and looks like a starfish, even to the dent in the middle. But it's the most dangerous thing in the Universe. Mostly it just floats around paying no attention to anything; it doesn't even seem to see what's around it. But if you happen to come too close and attract its attention, wow-ee, look out! They figure it has radar-like sensors on each of its five tips, for if it wants to it can listen to a man sneezing two light years away. You've heard about ships disappearing without a trace? They're on the Taco-grav, just talking away, and suddenly there's silence and you know the Elf-star got 'em. And nobody's really passed close to it and come back to tell. Once a star went nova from getting too close, and its whole planetary system was wiped out just like that!" He snapped his fingers to illustrate. "It was a close call for Pat and me. We were thinking of trading with one of its inner planets that year. You never know."

"How can you tell what this Elf-star looks like if no one who has gotten close has ever lived to tell about it?" asked the Prince.

"They figured it out," said Rodrigo. "Obviously no one is going to be able to sneak up on it and take its picture with a camera. They can't use radio detection systems on it either because it just back-tracks down the waves and wipes out the source. So they had to use the most modern science."

"Why don't they just shoot the Elf-star and get it over with," shrilled Harp.

"Shhhh! Not so loud." warned Pat. "You notice that we're not exactly shouting. Though there isn't supposed to be much danger here on this back-water planet, for we are pretty far from its path, you never know what it can understand and how far it listens when it happens to be listening. And you don't know how many languages it understands or what makes it mad, so it's better to be on the safe side and not say bad things about it or threaten it. They say you don't have to say real good things about it to be on the safe side, but some people do so for insurance. Of course no one wants to get it mad deliberately."

"How do you know if it's coming at you?"

"They calculate its path by oblique statistical recording of the abnormalities it causes as it goes along. They hear of a planet split down the middle, or of interplanetary dust that gets sucked up and disappears. The weirdest is when a twin to a star or planet just appears out of nowhere. And there was once a black hole that suddenly turned right into a nebula; that doesn't just happen naturally. You can hear all the observers yacking over the tacograv when they're in its path, warning each other, putting down transmission blackouts, all shipping frozen. Sometimes the damn thing (excuse me, I didn't mean that) drifts right by an intelligent planet and nothing happens. It just doesn't seem to notice, or if it does, it doesn't care."

"Can't you keep your voice down?" growled Rodrigo. "I don't want to get into trouble because of your big mouth."

"It's magic," said Harp reverently, "I've heard of magic."

"Don't meddle in what doesn't concern you," advised Rodrigo. He sidled over to the port that connected the cabin with Tak's private viewing tank and opened it.

"Got any more of that good stuff in there?" But there was no answer, so he poked his head through the hole.

"Phew-ee," he groaned. "It's hot. Look, the old bastard is sound asleep. He's floating around with all his arms spread out and both eyes shut. Shut off the ceiling projector, it's a waste of power."

Harp stuck his head in, too. "Hey, wake up," he shouted. "What's the matter with you?"

Tak must have heard, for some of his tentacles began a slow swimming motion and one eye partly opened; it had a peculiar evil look as though he resented having been wakened from his nap. He answered, gurgling horribly as though he were drowning.

"Right away, I'll be out right away. Didn't realize it was so late. Prepare the chart table, full speed astern...no, I mean neutral!" It was evident that he had been drinking his own gin very heavily, and the humans began to laugh. But Pat remembered that they needed the tank for the next hot water customer.

"Jesus, how long will it take to sober him up?" he asked. But no one had any idea, since a drunken Radial was outside their experience. Harp was willing to let him sleep it off until he remembered that his own liquor supply was dependant on Tak's ability to walk back to the Imbalancia.

So they decided to cool him down, which should get his attention, and to this end Pat pulled a lever that opened a drain between the hot and cold tanks. They settled down to wait, reminiscing about Earth and Harp's adventures with the scientific mind, with descriptions of Irma, Miss Squieze and Miss Constable, as well as Dr. Fish. The Black Ship's crew had never seen them and showed much interest. You may be sure that Dr. Fish's beauty lost much in the telling. Everyone was careful not to make the obvious remarks about the anatomy of Miss Squeeze as the Prince had informed them that they were engaged. They discussed the problem of how to get her out of Dr. Fish's clutches.

"If I could only get a message to her," he lamented. "Harp could deliver it." But Harp refused; nothing would induce him to return to captivity. He also opined that if the prince were to go back alone he might not be made prisoner but would probably not be able to reach her, locked as she was in Dr. Fish's Fastar. Harp thought that the best thing to do was for the prince to get back to Earth and return with an army. Pat and Rodrigo politely refrained from mentioning that the prince had no army.

But Red Pat had an inspiration. "We're outlaws anyway. We can raid them! What can two scientists and a bunch of women do against four men, even if Harp's one of us?"

They were all pretty well oiled, and when Tak's voice came from the tank to show he was awake, and they found that Harp's space suit was finally dry, they assembled themselves (Harp having exchanged his royal garb for common wear on the insistence of the prince) and prepared to sally forth.

The voice from the tank restrained them. "That was a terrible picture and not worth my best water-weed gin! You two, dress up my earthman properly and find him some gloves. I'm taking him back to Earth as soon as you Vandals have finished kidnaping the princess. When you've got her, you'd better head for Earth right away; you never know what kind of alarm they may be able to raise. It might be more dangerous for you to remain here than chancing the Elf-star. As for me, I'm tired of all of you and tired of making gin. It's going right down my drain into the ground as soon as I can get home. Then I'll take Harp back to Earth. I'm the chauffeur of the new high speed Crystal Changer belonging to the head of the Society. I'll just borrow it (they'll never miss it, busy as they are watching for the Elf-star) and be waiting at my door to pick up Harp as soon as you finish playing with him."

Tak's voice changed to the overbearing tone which Harp knew was meant for him. "I'll take you back to Earth and be rid of you in spite of the Elf-star, and then I'll not have to listen to your complaining during my Bridge game." His voice became plaintive again as he addressed the porno merchants. "That picture of yours wasn't worth a full bottle of gin and now I'm cold all over. I'm going home to warm up and get ready." They could hear him sloshing out the back door of the tank and groaning as he started to compress himself into his space suit.

Rodrigo let down the gangplank. They waited until they heard the Radial's noisy departure and then prepared to set out themselves, armed with flashlights, knives, wrenches and bits of chain, with their helmets down to disguise their faces. They checked to make sure all the tanks were empty of voyeurs, turned out the lights, tottered down the gangplank and lumbered out single file across the pebbles toward the unsuspecting delegates.

LIBERATION

Red Pat was the leader; it should have been the prince but he was so excited that he could do little more than gibber. Next came Harp, with Rodrigo behind to keep him from lagging and straying. It was not long before they reached the chute leading up to the delegates' pressure chamber, which was only large enough to hold two at a time.

Pat laid out the plan of attack. The prince and Harp were to enter first; Brute was to secure the doorway leading to Dr. Fish's Fastar, and Harp was to distract the others with accounts of his miraculous escape. The Black Ship's crew were then to burst in and make their demands known. Harp, as the least dependable fighter, would escort Miss Squieze to the Black Ship, leaving the others to make a strategic retreat as best they could. They would take all the space suits with them to prevent pursuit, as the delegates were still under the impression that they would die beyond the air lock without their suits.

At the foot of the chute leading to the delegates' cell they all hyperventilated a little to build up their courage. Harp and the prince climbed into the pressure chamber and from there entered the main room without difficulty, and no comment was made about the fact that their helmets were undone as they crawled out. They were welcomed effusively by the three delegates and Dr. Fish whom they found peacefully playing Bridge.

That broke up the game. Al suggested green tea and some green brownies. Harp expressed his thanks and the prince sat down casually in the doorway of the Fastar with one leg hanging over each side. He knew that Miss Squieze would not lock him out but was not sure of Miss Constable.

Then Pat and Rodrigo burst in, to the consternation of the Bridge players, and taking advantage of the confusion the prince called Harp over to sit in the doorway in his place while he climbed inside the Fastar. He emerged almost at once leading the blushing Miss Squieze by the hand, and motioning Harp out of the way, helped her into the room. Miss Constable looked out after them in alarm.

"You too," ordered Red Pat, laying back his helmet, and stepped forward to help Miss Constable through the port hole. She was thinner than Miss Squieze and slipped through without assistance. The delegates stared at the shaggy appearance of the interlopers, and the prince thought he had better make introductions all around. After that was finished, Harp dragged Irma's space suit off its hook and the prince started buckling his bride-to-be into it.

That brought loud protests from Miss Constable and Dr. Fish, who shouted something about Miss Squieze being on contract. The others only watched the goings-on with great interest. Red Pat now sat down in the Fastar doorway just in case any of the women should make a bolt for it.

"His Highness intends to marry this young lady," he said in a soft and reasonable tone, and what was visible of his mouth through his red beard was set in a pleasant smile. "I am the captain of the Black Ship, and by right of my office will perform the marriage ceremony immediately upon embarking. I hope none of you will stand in the way of her nuptual preferment." Here his smile enlarged itself into sentimentality. "Just think! She will soon become a Princess!" He had obviously been reading the better sort of Romance novels during his long boring space voyages.

Miss Squieze and Harp were ushered into the pressure chamber by the prince and Rodrigo, and the door was latched behind them. The prince should have been the next to go, but here everything changed. Red Pat's gentlemanly tones disappeared; he advanced into the center of the room with a buccaneer swagger and assigned the puzzled prince to take his place guarding the door.

"You didn't think we were going to be satisfied with taking only one girl, did you?" His sneer was masterly and he advanced upon the lovely Eustacia. She gave a terrified squeal and hid behind Wiener, clutching him from behind in a paralyzing hold with her arms around his neck. As though on cue Irma let out a yelp and, ducking behind Al, tangled her fingers in his hair with a death grip. At the same time Miss Constable began to scream. But there was nowhere for her to hide, as the Prince was too awkwardly placed in the doorway for her to get behind him.

This was a facer for the pirates: not only was the prince beginning to protest, but the two best looking women were not to be captured without a battle, and both Al and Wiener would perhaps prove to be fair fighters if they could get loose from the girls they planned to protect. They were both already beginning to growl. There was no one left for the pirates to abduct except Miss Constable. Pat and Rodrigo looked at each other in a resigned sort of way; she was at least thirty-five, and thin besides.

Pat spoke placatingly to her. "The princess will need a chaperon for the short time before she is married. Then she will need a bridesmaid. After that I have no doubt she will appoint you as her lady-in-waiting."

The argument was mighty thin, but then they had not taken Miss Constable's nature into account. A warm heart beat beneath her starchy exterior; she was also acquainted with the better sort of Romance novel. Though she knew perfectly well that this was an abduction planned with evil intent she pretended that it was a sort of invitation to tea, and even started to titter in a lady-like way, batting her eyes after the manner of Scarlett O'Hara. Who can blame her? Being dragged off into a life of sin was much preferable to a low-paid career under the thumb of Dr. Fish. She climbed agreeably into the other space suit and crawled with the prince into the empty pressure chamber.

Pat and Rodrigo, finally in the minority and hampered by

their awkward suits, were keeping an eye on Al and Wiener who might suddenly work themselves loose from the females and attack while the pirates were waiting their turn at the exit. It looked as though Wiener would soon be free, for Dr. Fish was relaxing her grip preparatory to giving the abductors a piece of her mind. Rodrigo bared his teeth and snarled, advancing toward her. The result was satisfactory; she threw herself again on Wiener, this time from the front, effectively blocking his view and engaging his arms and hands as he automatically clutched her to him. The two pirates made a clean and easy get-away.

They found the wedding party waiting at the foot of the Black Ship's gangway, their helmets thrown back to the night air; the men were proud and excited by the success of their foray. The six of them mounted laughing into the belly of the ship and removed their cumbersome space suits. Red Pat started at once shuffling through trunks and boxes on the hunt for a book of Common Prayer. There were plenty of black market Gideon bibles which the ship had contracted to drop off at every planetary stop, as well as to scatter them throughout the Imbalancia, but it was a long time before he found the words for the marriage ceremony. He finally stumbled on them in a book of interplanetary etiquette that the ship's chandlers had urged on him at the commencement of his first voyage.

Meanwhile the girls had done what they could to make Miss Squeeze look like a bride. The fact that she was already dressed in white, albeit a nurse's uniform, was a good beginning. A length of unused white message printer tape was curled into festoons for her hair and a bundle of artificial seaweed, trade goods for some sea creatures, was decorated with curls of white and pink tape until it almost looked like a bouquet. The result was satisfactory and her beatific smile made her ensemble complete.

Miss Constable had also created a corsage for herself from seaweed and tape, and the two ladies had persuaded the reluctant Rodrigo to give up his treasured ear ring to bend into a wedding band. The prince, with Harp, whom he had chosen as his best man, had been sent into an empty cabin so as not to watch the proceedings.

All was ready as they waited for Pat to find the vital book. Rodrigo suddenly snapped his fingers, which made Miss Constable jump. Her poise and dreadful calm were the result of long training and experience in the handling of the sick and insane, and bore no relation at all to her internal condition, which consisted of a thumping heart with fits of dizziness. She was far more excited than the bride-to-be, who was enjoying her elopement as a sort of lark, whereas Miss Constable had many tangible fears.

Rodrigo grabbed her by the wrist and urged her not ungently to follow him down the corridor which led to the passengers' staterooms. He stopped at one of the doors, opened it and pushed her inside. Her heart thumped so strongly that she could hardly breathe; her legs seemed to give way beneath her. He stepped in behind her and shut the door. It was a large room with a double bed, a few chairs, a wardrobe and a table. The lamp was unplugged. She could feel his hot breath on the back of her neck. I must submit, she thought. There is no other way out for me. She said good-bye to her virginity as though it were a bird flying away, and sighed.

"Don't make any noise," he said gruffly. He walked over to the wardrobe and flung open the doors. "The sheets and pillows are in here. Hurry and make up the bed for them, and then dust a little. They'll need a bridal suite. The towels are in the cupboard in the bathroom. When you're done with that, fix up a stateroom for yourself two doors down the hall. Put on plenty of blankets; we always lower the heat at night."

She was extremely rattled at the change in the anticipated agenda, and stood with uneven breath and hands flapping uselessly as Rodrigo prepared to leave. He was chuckling to himself in the most distressing way, almost lasciviously, and she had the unwelcome impression that he had guessed what had been going through her mind while they had been standing close together. He left without shutting the door and she could hear his laughter all the way down the corridor. But she steadied herself, and remembering that she was both a nurse and a bridesmaid, set to work. A shout just before she was finished brought her running down the hall to the sitting room. All was in readiness. Pat had made a sort of platform out of a box and stood on it gazing benignly down at his congregation. Rodrigo played the role of both father and choir, and sang an original if somewhat gruff rendition of "Here Comes the Bride." The ring had been reluctantly entrusted to Harp. The groom looked worried. Miss Constable preceded the happy and confident bride up to the edge of the platform and left her with the prince, who seemed to be suffering from some terrible anxiety.

"Is something wrong?" whispered Miss Squieze.

"My darling," answered the prince, choking back a sob, "I must ask you an important question before we are married."

"What is it?"

"I should have inquired before. It's all my fault! Darling, forgive me! The question is, do you know how to swim?"

"Of course I can swim! Why?"

"Do you have any serious objection to swimming in public without any clothes on?"

"Not at all," She chuckled pleasantly. "My father used to take us to a nudist colony in Wisconsin during the summers. I learned to swim there. I can also sail a boat!"

'Then everything's all right. Let's get on with the wedding!"

Pat leaned down from the platform and asked the bride her full name.

"Barbie Cushion Squieze," she murmured in a modest little voice. The prince was electrified at the sound of her name and jumped back in horror!

"Are you one of that crew?" he shouted. "Are you related to the founder of the Aubudon Society? My God, say you're not! I can't bear it!"

"We're only a degenerate branch," she whispered soothingly. "We were never members of the Society. My ancestors weren't even environmentalists; they only made armaments and the less successful members worked as lobbyists for tobacco companies.

"Well, that's all right then," said the prince, relieved. "You understand that I could not ally myself to conservationists. What would my sisters say?"

The wedding continued and Miss Squieze became Princess Barbie. Everyone clapped, handshakes and kisses were exchanged, and even the surprised Harp was included in the goodwill. Then they all stood around nibbling on pieces of Hershey bars which the princess had cut for them, pretending it was cake, and taking polite sips out of their soda cans until Rodrigo said, glancing sideways at Miss Constable, "Why don't you two go down the corridor and see what a nice room Miss Constable has fixed up for you? Show them, Constable."

They passed from sight, but not from hearing. The newlyweds spoke in hushed tones.

"I can't call you Prince any more, now that we are married," twittered the bride. "What should I call you? Should I say Robert?"

"No. You'd better call me Brute," was the affectionate reply.

Miss Constable returned and the four of them stood there stiffly, working on their chocolate and not looking at one another. Finally the pirates turned to stare at Miss Constable. They both looked at Harp and then at each other.

"We've had a hard day," said Pat blandly. "We all need our sleep. Harp, why don't you go home, get some rest and prepare for your trip to Earth if you are still determined to go. Tak must be waiting for you. I'll help you into a space suit. We'll give you one of the good ones."

Harp zipped up and bade them good-night, and Pat gave him a sheaf of Hershey bars as a parting gift. He started to eat one right away. Then he tottered down the gangplank and the last thing he heard from above was Rodrigo asking Miss Constable what her first name was.

THE LIBERATION OF HARP

It did not take long for Harp to travel between the two ships and clamber up Tak's chute. It had been a little cold outdoors and he found the pressure chamber comfortably warm. The door to Tak's room was wide open; the water on the floor had ceased steaming and the tap had stopped leaking. The Radial was already dressed in his many-armed suit and carried the Anebit coiled up in a tentacle. It was no longer encased in a plastic bag and the lid that covered its top was hanging open like Harp's helmet.

Harp had not had a good look at it before. It was the shape of a caved in bottle and seemed to be made of reddish brown rubber. Tak held it out for his inspection. A single eye peered back at him. It watched him closely and reminded him of his second grade teacher who had looked at him the same way. The teacher usually made a mark in her notebook after each such look and he felt that the Anebit was doing the same, remembering all the awful things he had done. He lowered his eyes.

"Come on," ordered Tak, and crammed the three of them into the pressure chamber and locked the door. Then he undid another door and ushered Harp into a shining space apparently enclosed in glass, for he could see some of the lights of the Imbalancia twinkling through its sides and bottom.

"You are extremely fortunate to be invited to ride in this magnificent invention. It does not belong to me; I have borrowed it for the occasion. Mind you do not break or scratch anything. I do not want to see it marred by your clumsiness before I return it to its owner, who does not know it is being borrowed. I am now going to retire into the navigational tank over there and you must make yourself comfortable where you are. I have left you a pot of cooked water-weed and a bottle of alcohol, for I have not the slightest idea how long the trip will take, never having driven the Crystal Changer before. I am also leaving the Anebit in your charge. You may look into its eye for its amusement, but do not speak to it or touch it. And do not take your space suit off. Now close your helmet and get ready for the worst!" Tak withdrew into the navigator's tank, which was hot and steamy; Harp could scarcely see him through the glass.

The Anebit slouched beside Harp on the floor and gazed at him without blinking. He inspected the supplies Tak had left him and took out a small pinch of sea-weed. He hesitated before eating it and offered it first to the Anebit, which snapped its lid shut in refusal. "Excuse me," he said. There was nothing for him to sit on. The floor was covered with a kind of transparent matting, not too hard, so he sat there and then lay down on it and took a little nip from the bottle.

He had no idea how long he had slept but when he woke the sky outside the ship was black, ornamented with a few stars. He sat up and looked around. Tak was illuminated inside his tank by a dim light. The Anebit beside him gave off just enough of a glow for him to see a little. It's useful after all, he thought, and moved over to sit closer to it for company.

It was not watching him now; its eye pointed toward the stars. So he looked, too. It was not an interesting sight; everything went by much too fast in multi-colored streaks. The only things that stood still were the very distant stars, and even they changed their positions or disappeared suddenly from time to time. He opened his helmet and spoke crossly to the Anebit, but it paid him no attention and did not take its single eye off the stars.

While Harp was gazing blankly at the lights and streaks in front of him, out of the corner of his eye he noticed a little pink thing like a hand pressed momentarily against the transparent wall of the Crystal Changer. At the same time the Anebit gave a sudden start beside him. What can that be, he thought. Is there someone out there? But the hand was instantly gone and he did not think about it again.

He noticed that Tak inside his transparent tank was refreshing himself with the water-weed gin that he had brought in a large canister for his own use. It looked like a good idea, so Harp took a few good gulps from his own bottle, tightened his helmet and went back to sleep.

When he awoke again it was to find his helmet full of mushed, evil smelling water-weed.

"Who has made this terrible mess?" Even through his helmet he could easily hear Tak's angry roar.

"I was sick," said Harp piteously. He removed his helmet. The whole room was spattered with the same vile substance. Harp did not wish to take the blame for all the other vomit as well as his own mess, but refrained from explaining that he, with his small size, could not possibly have been responsible for such a quantity. He could see that Tak was one of those drinkers who retain no memory of their own indiscretions and at the same time allow no one else to retain one, either.

"Disgusting," scolded Tak. "But it won't take long to clean up. Give me your helmet." He handed it over and it was subjected to a violent spray of hot water from a hose attached to the navigational tank. Then it was handed back, clean and hot, and Harp was instructed to put it back on and fasten it down firmly. That accomplished, Tak hosed down the interior of the Crystal Changer with a blast that obscured Harp's view for several seconds and knocked him down. When the air cleared again the inside of the ship was sparkling. He lifted his helmet back onto its hinge. The Anebit was lying on its side near him, clean like everything else, its lid firmly shut.

"What happened?" he asked.

"Cleaned and flushed! Flushed and clean! All the refuse is out in space. A little fact I would not care to communicate to the Conscience of the Aubudon Society, considering their policy on pollution. But the Crystal Changer does not have recycling facilities; one is expected to hold down one's dinner or not travel at all." He laughed enthusiastically at his own joke, body and tentacles trembling in happy unison within the confines of his space suit.

"Harp, my boy." he boomed. "You don't have to get out at Earth. You can come back home with me; it won't matter if you've changed your mind. We can go back. Perhaps you won't even like Earth. You are welcome to live in my refrigerator, or you can move in with the Vandals; they want you, too."

But Harp muttered "No thank-you," and the ship started to vibrate as it entered the Earth's atmosphere. They descended in silence for a considerable time and then landed easily in a clump of ornamental shrubs in one of the obscure corners of the National Cemetery. They had arrived back in Bostown with no real difficulty at all. For all his bizarre behavior, Tak was truly a wonderful navigator.

It was one of the quietest hours of the night; the landing went completely unnoticed except by some sleeping birds that chirped in alarm at the reflections of the moon on the faceted hull. As soon as Harp saw they were down he climbed out of his space suit and into the plastic tube which served as the exit lock. The tube was big enough for even the Radial to squeeze into, so after the valve closed Harp still had plenty of room to wave a vigorous silent farewell to his many-armed friend, who waved a tentacle in return. The starry view through the transparent walls of the ship had turned into a dark garden awaiting him, and he wiggled through the other end of the tube into the night air.

The wind outside chilled him; he had forgotten the hostile feeling of cold. But this was his home, it felt right, and when he turned back toward the Crystal Changer it was not so much in regret as to see how Tak would look inside his bubble. But the space-ship presented only the mirror image of his own body, which he could see shivering in the glass.

Then suddenly the ship was gone; there was not even an implosion as it left, only a nearly invisible crushed patch in the bushes and a slight hollow in the ground. The wax-like flowers on the surrounding bushes did not even quiver with its departure.

It was a moonlit spring night, cold but not freezing. The stars were bright and Harp looked at them with newly-found respect. Mixed with the smell of spring blossoms was the odor of the forest, for nearby was a bank planted with young spruce trees. But before further exploration he needed a drink. He pulled his bottle out of the yellow-spotted cumberbund with which he had decorated his new black coverall before the celebration of the royal wedding. It was the same bottle that Dr. Fish had given him long ago and he had preserved it through all his adventures. He searched for meaning in this fact as he took a fortifying gulp.

The drink warmed him and he threw his arms wide in welcome to his new freedom; he could now be himself in perfect liberty in his own land. He flung himself down on the spruce covered bank to savor the sensation.

Then he rolled onto his back and raised his chin to view the night sky. They were only twinkling little stars after all. Faces seemed to peep out at him behind and between the stars, but he drove these visions away with a scowl and a wave of one arm. He hoped momentarily that the Crystal Changer might be one of the bright points of light but he could not tell. Tak would never return, but he did not need him anyway.

Harp revelled again in his freedom to do what he wished, whether it be something or nothing. He shook his fist at Dr. Fish, whose beautiful face suddenly leered at him from near the moon, and laughed luxuriantly. Then he began to wonder if real eyes, eyes near the ground, might be watching him too, but dismissed the idea with another swig. Warm from the bottle and the happiness of being his own man again, he fell heavily asleep.

When he awoke it was near dawn and he felt as though he would shake to pieces from the cold. He got up painfully and drank to get warm again. Then he rose to his feet and, stretching, surveyed his kingdom. The first rays of the sun touched him obliquely and he fancied that they gave off heat.

"Now I know all about you, Sun," he said learnedly.

"Without you and your brothers life could not exist. It would be all dry and dark. You'd better be grateful too, you flowers." He kicked at a large Rhododendron in a friendly way, making some of the big purple flowers swing and scatter their drops on his elegant hand-sewn shies, another gift from the pirates. He slapped at the higher blooms with one hand, rejoicing in the cold shower of dew. Then he washed his joy down with a few swallows from the bottle, and felt the need for breakfast.

He walked briskly in the direction where civilization might be waiting and peered into the first open trash container that he came to. Sure that there was something delicious inside, he fumbled at a soft wrapped sack. He did not hear the approach of the Horsemen until they were behind him and it was too late to run.

"Well Sir," said their leader graciously. "Been up a bit late, haven't we. Missed the last tube home and sleeping it off in the grounds?"

Harp was not slow to take up this cue. In a superior tone and with even a slight gurgle in imitation of Tak he pronounced, "Unfortunately, officer, that is the case. If you will be good enough to show me the location of the return tube, I'll be off home. I was quite turned around and I've never passed a colder or more uncomfortable night; the ground is positively sodden."

"I'll show him the way," said one of the Horsemen. The others wheeled and trotted off, the sound of their horses' hooves receeding over the nearest hillock.

Harp looked up at the face of his guide and found him gazing down on him with a peculiar expression. "You can just point out the way. I'll find the tube myself," he said uneasily.

The officer grinned at him. It was a toothy grin. Harp noticed how large and white and strong his teeth looked in his weather-beaten face.

"I knew you right away," said the officer triumphantly, at the same time putting a cautionary hand on Harp's collar as he showed signs of slithering away. "All of a sudden you are a dressed up sharpie. Well, wherever you got those clothes it doesn't matter. Now lookit, I won't turn you in. You got a raw deal last time; I don't know how you survived. I was one of those who had to carry the others out (doctor's orders, you know) to the Lying-in-State house." He paused and looked thoughtfully into the air. When he looked back there was no trace of a smile on his face.

"I won't turn you in, never fear. Those doctors and all the other scientists can rot and I'll not lift a finger to help them. As for you, I'll send you back home on an expired ticket; the man who collects them at the tube entrance is a cousin of mine."

"But you don't understand," said Harp. "I don't want to go home, I want to stay here. I came back on purpose."

"You're crazy!"

"This is the only place where I can get a drink," whimpered Harp.

"Booze got you for good?" asked the Horseman sympathetically.

"Christ, yes, I couldn't live a week on the outside. Please let me stay, Sir. I'll do anything you say." the practiced whine came easily. He sniffed and mumbled pitifully.

"O.K., O.K., it's your business. In that case go get yourself a Ghoul's license. I've done what I can for you; it's up to you now." He started digging in his pockets, looking for something to write with. The reins lay slack on the horse's neck. Harp, who was gazing at the near eye of the horse, spoke timidly.

"Can I hold your horse for you while you look?"

"Sure, but don't make any fast moves. Have you ever held a horse before?"

"I've seen it done." He tenderly grasped the rein and looked up at the huge tame creature. The horse blew gently through its nose and a tiny warm puff of air tickled the hairs on Harp's neck. He timidly raised a hand and touched the horse's cheek. Then he remembered that he had heard horses liked to eat sugar. He still had the piece of sugar Dr. Fish had given him before he had gone away with Tak; it had survived all his adventure and was resting now in its waterproof pouch in his pocket. He tore the packet open and offered the sugar on the flat of his hand the way he was supposed to. The horse nibbled it up happily. I'll always remember this, he thought.

"That's enough." said the Horseman. "Go take this note to the right door this time or you'll get into trouble." He tightened the reins, touched the sleek side of his mount with his heel and cantered off without a backward look.

Harp tipped up his bottle and finished it. He hurried across the cemetery, meeting only a few early rising scavengers; they edged away from his purposeful approach with downcast but observant eyes. He found himself the only mendicant standing before the red door and waited until opening time, stamping impatiently while his guts ached from hunger and thirst. By then the line had grown like a tail behind him. But he was the first to be let in, the first to have his hand tattooed, to have a cup handcuffed to his wrist. The first to be handed a sandwich and be poured a measured ounce of whiskey. He was even commiserated with and examined in a cursory way by a cheerful intern.

"Liver's damaged a bit, but nothing you can't live with if you're careful," he said and pinned on the coveted badge. "All right, man, go!"

Harp spent the morning patrolling his new domain, lying on a bench in the warm sun, sleeping, getting up, drinking all he wanted, crunching potato chips and above all, talking.

It was a beautiful shining day. Audiences collected around him whenever he felt lively enough to stand up. They were attracted by his unusual dress. Coins and tokens came his way continually; he used some for drink, some to buy potato chips and even had enough left to jingle in his pockets.

"Listen, you people. I've been out among the stars, I've ridden in space ships, talked to creatures you wouldn't believe, with arms all over them, creatures that appear and disappear into thin air. And I fooled them all. They tried to keep me prisoner but I escaped. I've know royalty, fought with pirates. They make booze up there out of seaweed and they're sex-crazed. You should see the things they do. The ground is all covered with diamonds and rubies. I could have brought some home, but I forgot. You can just pick them up and fill your pockets. Let me tell you...."

The faces smiled around him, though some of the watchers cackled and jeered. This made him angry. They threw coins and tokens, and he drank and slept all day.

When he awoke again it was getting dark. He sat up. A man dressed in filthy rags was sitting on a bench nearby and looked at him dully but calculatingly. Harp cleared his throat and spat. He had lost his bottle somewhere so he felt in his pocket for the reassuring tokens and coins. They were still there so he was satisfied to wait a few minutes and get his bearings before going in search of the beer wagon.

"This place isn't safe," he said morosely to his new companion. "You can just be sitting there minding your own business, and boom! they kidnap you and put you in a space ship and send you to the other end of the Universe to fend for yourself. They torture you, too. Have you ever had an intravenous injection?"

"Go to Hell," snarled his neighbor.

Harp got up and went in search of a beer vendor but they had disappeared into the twilight, striped awnings, big aprons and all. It was really dark now and beginning to get quite cold again. He shivered and mumbled in self-pity as he reflected that it only stayed sunny in the cemetery for a little while.

Then he heard the angry shouts of the distant Horsemen as they rounded up the Ghouls for the night, lashing with their whips at the ones who were too slow to run. Harp could hear the scuffling and the groans and above all the pounding of the hooves. He resolved not to be one of the captured and fled around a hill and into a plantation, the same spicy smelling spruce grove he had crouched in early that morning.

After a while the sounds of hunting abated and he heard the distant clang of the doors as the Ghouls were locked up for the night in their ashy underground home. For a moment he felt abandoned and lonely, but then he pictured the ashes dirtying his new clothes and resolved to put off going to bed as long as possible; he even considered spending the night in the damp air, clutching himself for warmth, looking up at the friendly sky which was now black without moon or stars. He wished he had a drink and thought perhaps there was a bottle hidden among the men in the ashes. But he put off bedtime a little longer; the thought of the nearness and peevishness of the others oppressed him.

His plan to remain in the open was doomed to failure; the cold and the need for a drink were too much for him, and he got up drearily to look for the path that led to the Ghouls' ashy basement. He walked with difficulty in the dark, sometimes straying off the path and tripping over stone markers or tangling his feet in flowers and sinking into the fresh turned earth.

Finally a dark shape rose before him and a feeling of warmth in the air told him that he was nearing a building. He put out his hand and moved forward until he touched the warm bricks. Then he felt along the wall until he came to a corner, followed it around blindly, and located an opened door leading down a long flight of steps to a vestibule illuminated by a soft glowing light. He walked down the stairs until he reached the bottom. It was hot, almost suffocatingly airless. In front of him was a large double door without handles at the foot of a steep incline. It was a metal door, battered and badly fitting, for he could see flickering lights through the cracks around its edges and he heard a confused roaring behind it as of many voices quarreling.

I need that drink, he thought, and stumbled down the incline and pressed his hand against the door. The burning heat of the metal warned him of the danger within, but his shuffling impetus was so great that the doors swung open at his touch and he was sucked willy-nilly into the roaring flames of the crematorium.

RETURN TO THE IMBALANCIA

The omniscient Elf-star, normally so destructive, had this day chosen to exercise one of its more unusual talents. Able to destroy or create at will with its five-lobed brain, it had rested its little star points lightly upon the Crystal Changer and then left to find purpose or amusement elsewhere.

Now there were two Crystal Changers with duplicate contents: two Harps, two Radials, two Anebits, all without harmful effect other than violent indigestion and some memory loss. Of course there were slight differences; as two leaves, however well cloned, are never exactly alike.

Now that we have learned what happened to the original Harp, staggering in his feckless way straight to his doom, we must follow his younger brother Harp, as well as the extra Tak and the extra Anebit, riding through space innocently unaware of what had happened, all very lucky that the Elf-star had not taken a dislike to them.

Harp did not feel so well, not really the same. He attributed it to having waked up with his helmet full of green vomit. He undid it angrily, and took the thing off and flung it into a corner. The whole interior of the Crystal changer was likewise splattered with verdent debris, and Tak appeared to have passed out in his navigational tank. Harp crawled over and pounded on the side of the tank with his slimy gloved fist until Tak awoke. The first thing the Radial did was to fling off his own dangling helmet and douse it in the hot water. His character had either changed temporarily during his period of drunken sleep or else his temper had taken a setback.

"Arrgh!" he roared, and slapped savagely at Harp. Luckily his tentacles were not yet completely under his control and they missed Harp by several inches.

Tak sat back at this and appeared to think while Harp watched him as a cornered mouse watches a playful cat. The expression in the Radial's eye revealed that he did not think of him as a friend; he did not even seem to recognize him. Harp cowered against the opposite wall, squeezing himself in between two instruments that looked important. Perhaps even the obstreperous Tak would hesitate to damage the working parts of a ship that he had borrowed without permission.

But Tak did not attack him again. Instead he pointed imperiously at the Anebit which had collapsed on the floor in a small pool of oil with its lid tightly closed. The trembling Harp picked it up and brought it to him. The Radial accepted it carefully and dunked it in his tank, shook it a little and then patted it on the back, or stomach, until it opened its lid. He dipped it again and looked inside with first one eye and then the other. He spent considerable time examining it, then handed it back to Harp and said to him in a soft clumsy voice, as though he were unused to speaking, "Excuse me, little cold disagreeable creature, I have temporarily lost my memory. But some of it has now returned. This is the Crystal Changer and you and I were going somewhere in it, were we not?"

"To Earth, to return me where I belong," said Harp nervously.

"Why would I do that?" was the puzzled reply. Harp attempted to explain Tak's strongly held belief that endangered species should never be removed from their environments, only to discover that the Radial had no idea where or what Earth was.

"I am very sick," he groaned. "I feel that I need medical care. So we are going back to Vpor where the Anebit tells me that all the best doctors are located."

"Stop!" cried Harp, horrified by visions of a planet covered in hot water and steam. "There are good doctors even nearer than Vpor. Doctors and nurses, too. Let's go back to the Imbalancia; that's where you really belong anyway, because you're the chief navigator."

The Radial consulted the Anebit again. "Yes, of course, you're right. I am needed at the Imbalancia. It slipped my mind for the moment. But what is this disgusting mess?" He indicated the green slime smeared inside the ship's interior.

"The Anebit did it," said Harp, beginning to catch on to Tak's infirmity and feeling that anything he could do to reduce the Anebit's prestige in the eyes of Tak would be to his own advantage. After all it was not as though the calculator were alive and had any feelings.

"Well, the Anebit can clean it up then," said Tak, shaking it crossly. With one eye close to the lens for instructions, he flipped some switches and a roar of steam filled the chamber. Harp ran to retrieve his helmet and pulled it back on just in time to avoid being scalded. The steam scoured the whole area and when Harp ventured to open his helmet a crack he found the cabin spotless, as though it had just emerged from a terrestrial dishwasher. Left uncleaned were the inside of his helmet and his own face. He repaired this condition with his beautiful dotted silk cumberbund which he dragged out from inside his space suit.

He found Tak adjusting instruments slowly with the aid of the Anebit. "We'll be back at the Imbalancia in no time," said the Radial cheerfully. "Wonderful little machine, this Crystal Changer. I can't think where I bought it." He shook the Anebit, but it did not give him an answer to this question.

"Probably doesn't even know, due to spending all its life in my pocket instead of being outside where it can see everything going on around it. I asked it is name and it said 'pocket-piece'. Isn't' that strange? It thinks it's a watch, and so it is, in a way. From now on I'll wear it on one of my wrists." He wrapped it around one limb and tucked its lid through the hole at its other extremity. It caught and held and he slid the Anebit up the tentacle until it fitted snugly.

"Looks very well on me," he said, turning the tentacle this way and that so he could see the Anebit from all sides.

"Very handsome," agreed Harp, who would do or say nearly anything to humor the Radial into a swift return to the Imbalancia. He looked into the Anebit's eye, which was no longer protected by its lid, and thought he detected a curiously distressed expression.

"Sometimes I think they keep these computers in a refrigerator when they are not in use. It keeps them fresh," he ventured. "They can stand only so much heat."

"Oh, very well," sulked the deprived Tak. "Then you take it. But leave it alone and don't play with it. It's mine."

Harp accepted his charge and laid it down carefully in the spot where Tak had placed it at the beginning of the voyage. Its lid was now clamped firmly shut.

The return to the Imbalancia was slow. Harp, slouched on the Crystal Changer's floor, went to sleep several times from boredom. He was also extremely hungry but there seemed to be nothing to eat aboard the ship. His stomach growled and occasionally spots appeared before his eyes. Fortunately there was water for drinking out of the steam jet; he collected it in his helmet and let it cool. He could also wash his face when he wanted to, but he longed for food. He found a bottle of liquid in a corner that smelled like cleaning fluid. He mentioned his need for food repeatedly to the Radial, who showed little sympathy.

"Live off your fat deposits or absorb light," he recommended.

Eventually the Anebit opened its lid and Harp carried it over and held it up before the Radial's eye, for it closed each time Tak touched it, and the peevish little computer guided them back to the Imbalancia.

First there was a crash followed by a long moment of silence. Then Tak climbed out of his tank and opened the door and there they were: in Tak's pressure chamber. Another door led to Tak's big room; the floor deep in water and steam. The little rubber boat was floating not far from the door. Clutching the

Anebit, which he had carried out under his arm, and paying no attention to what Tak was doing, Harp climbed aboard and paddled over to his refrigerator shelf.

He climbed up with difficulty, pulling the boat behind him, not forgetting to secure the paddle in its slot, and laid the Anebit in its usual place next to a plastic wrapped package. After removing his space suit he hunted for something to eat. He found some frozen spinach which he chewed without first warming it, and three very hard Hershey bars. Next he washed his space suit by dipping it in the hot water over the edge on the shelf and hung it on a projecting spur of ice to dry. Then, his housekeeping completed, he lay down on his practical little rubber boat, now pleasantly warm, and went to sleep, secure at last upon a solid shelf, resting on solid stilts, supported on solid ground. It would have been more satisfactory to have lain on Earth but that dream was slipping away from him due to Tak's uncooperative vagueness, and besides he was unwilling to go through anything like that again.

When he awoke his mouth tasted a little of raw weeds but his breath was clean and fresh, which seemed odd. He lay back idly planning his breakfast and thinking over his recent adventures. Pleasant though it was to lie on his inflated mattress and cool his toes on ice and think about feasting on cooked greens and to reflect upon his uniqueness and his ability to escape unscathed from any sort of vicissitude, he was still aware that something was missing. What could it be?

Was he lonely? Tak, previous to his lapse of memory, had been a companion, though not quite a mother, not quite a father, nor yet a boss. He remembered affectionately that he had been allowed to throw chunks of ice at him with impunity. The crazy new Tak would probably not allow such liberties. There was one sort of companionship ruined. He sighed. Yes, he was lonely.

There was another comfort he missed; it had something to do with drinking out of a bottle. But he couldn't remember what it was. Probably the voyage in the Crystal Changer had affected his memory as it had Tak's. He tried to think back to see if his mind was in good working order. He recollected the beginning of his travels. There he was in the Fastar, hungry and sore. He remembered the cruel Dr. Fish and his traveling companions the monkey and the cat. And there were two nurses; one was nicer than the other and would have been kind to him if she had not been afraid of Dr. Fish.

Then there was the prince. He was not exactly a friend but had sometimes slipped him food on the sly. And there was Al next door who was sometimes nice to him. Where were they? Somewhere nearby? He did not remember anything else clearly. He gave up and boiled some greens in the hot steaming water. Tak was down in the pool somewhere, for the water bubbled up from time to time and seemed more tumulteous than normal.

Harp set his cooking can onto the ice pack to cool and hauled the raft over so he could squat on it in comfort while he ate. The Anebit was still lying on the ledge where he had left it. While he was waiting for his food to cool he looked closely at the curious calculator. Its lid was open in what he thought might be a yearning sort of way, so he said "hello" and drew it a little nearer for companionship. It wiggled a bit when he touched it and he glanced quickly at the seething water to make sure that Tak was not watching, then rubbed the little fellow on its belly, or back, to see what would happen.

Just as he had hoped, it began to squirm happily. So he gave it a good scratching and tickling while it bounced around. He was careful not to let it bounce off the shelf into the water. He found this amusing for a while, but his mind drifted and the calculator became quiet. He noticed a funny thing. The plastic wrapped package next to it was also wiggling a little, as though it were trying to escape from its wrappings.

He glanced again at the bubbling indoor pond, and when he found that no angry eye was staring at him out of the steam he quickly unwound the plastic wrap. Out tumbled another Anebit, identical to the first, with its lid hanging open. He looked inside and the single eye stared out at him. Another glance at the water surface and he gave it a quick tickle. It was delighted, and squirmed about like the other one.

He had an idea. Perhaps an Anebit had feelings after all. If that was the case, maybe it was capable of feeling lonely, like him. He had no real friend but he could help the two Anebits; he laid them on their sides so their tops faced each other and their eyes could meet.

Having done this good deed, a great feeling of peace swept over him and he settled down to make a good meal of his boiled spinach. Where the other Anebit had come from he did not even question; he had come to accept the way things suddenly changed around him.

He left the Anebits alone to enjoy their own company and set out to make his quarters as agreeable as possible. First he assigned himself a toilet in one corner where everything could freeze solid. Previously he had used the waters below as one might have used a polluted stream, but he considered the condition of his own drinking supply as well as that of Tak. The melted ice from which he obtained his drinking water probably came from the same source, and he felt himself rather dirty in his habits and wondered why he had never thought of it before.

He chipped loose ice from the floor with his shoe and pushed it over the edge. Then he stood back and surveyed his work, and did not find it very satisfactory. He considered moving out but the thought of going back to the delegates and Dr. Fish was intolerable. He suddenly remembered the two friendly men in the Black Ship and he strained to recall the events connected to them. Finally he dredged out of his faulty memory the fact that he had been once offered a job by Pat and Rodrigo.

He gave a cry of joy and, not bothering to put on his soggy space suit, launched his little boat and paddled to the pressure chamber and climbed in. The four doors were unlabeled. Once led back into Tak's hot water room. He closed it and chose another at random, operating the mechanism that unsealed it.

It popped open and he found himself looking into the cabin of the CrystalChanger and tried the door nearly opposite. After a preliminary hissing it too popped open to reveal the Crystal

Changer again. He slammed that door shut and spun around suspiciously to the opposite one again. There could not possibly be two Crystal Changers, for he recalled that Tak had once told him that it was unique. It was possible that it had slipped away from one entrance and clamped onto the other while he had been walking across the air lock. Though he had not seen any living creature in either of the little ships, such was his awe of the Crystal Change that he did not put it past it to have switched doors of its own volition.

So he opened the first door again, but the glassy walled vehicle was still there. He shut the door hurriedly and resolved to return to his refrigerator immediately for a rest, feeling that there must be something wrong with him; perhaps too much space travel had made him sick. But of course he had forgotten which door he had come through. He cautiously opened one at random, and to his relief he found it led outside.

The chute was no longer attached and when he leaned out to see what was below he found that the distance to the ground was more than twenty feet. The Imbalancia had probably shifted a little. However, there were so many bumps and protrusions on the skin of the old ship that he was sure he could find enough hand holds to make a descent. He could see the Black Ship at an easy distance and heaved a sigh of relief.

But there was still something that nagged at his mind: he had to settle the mystery of the two Crystal Changers before he left. He pulled his head and shoulders back into the air lock and opened the two closed doors as simultaneously as possible. His scheme was successful; there really were two Crystal Changers. He crawled timidly inside one of them and found it just as he had left it: A few flecks of dry green vomit still clung to some rivet heads and his dirty cumberbund lay crumpled in a corner. The bottle of brown liquid lay against the wall.

He closed the door to the first ship and cautiously put one foot into the second one. It seemed just the same except for the absence of the cumberbund and the bottle. There were a few flecks of dry green vomit there too, but in different places.

Harp made his escape, and slammed that door firmly. He resolved never to approach either of the Crystal Changers again.

Instead he hauled his little rubber raft out of the water and stuffed it through the exit so that it tumbled down to the jewel-laden ground, where it would serve as a cushion in case he slipped during his descent. He did not bother to close the door leading to Tak's water room.

He found it easier to climb down than he had thought, and once on the ground he stood back and looked up to admire the precipitous route down which he had come. He could see the two Crystal Changers distinctly as two mirrored globes on either side of the exit. They looked very similar to the multi-faceted vehicle under which he and Al and Wiener had stood only a few days previously, back when he had still been an experimental animal. Though they had been unable to look through the shining walls and see what was inside, he now knew that they had been right in feeling they might be under observation.

He carried his boat underneath the Imbalancia where he thought it might lie out of sight, and sat down on it for a brief rest before heading toward the Black Ship.

A pair of strange looking birds, flying side by side, suddenly erupted with a loud whirring noise from directly over his head. He had never seen anything like them before: they had bodies shaped like ducks and were a smooth reddish brown color and seemingly had no feathers. Their flat round bills hung open as they flew, and their tiny almost invisible wings whirred as fast as those of a hummingbird. They headed straight out from the Imbalancia until they were only two small specks against the sky, then turned in formation and flew back almost to where they had started, nearly overhead. They dipped down to where he was sitting so that he could see them clearly, then clapped their bills loudly a few times, and mounting high again, turned left and flew rapidly along the side of the great ship until they disappeared from sight.

It took him a while to believe what he had seen, and when he realized that he had witnessed the escape of the two Anebits, for which he had no doubt been responsible by leaving the two doors open to the outside, he was glad that he was safe on the ground and near enough to the Black Ship to make a run for it when the Radial discovered his loss.

But for the moment he could not make a run for the Black Ship. It was broad daylight, or at least it was as broad as it could be with such a pale yellow sun; some of the planet inspectors were poking around in the middle distance along with some suited-up regulars, and Harp did not want to be collected by them while crossing the open space. He regretted that he had not brought his space suit for protection. He watched the creatures carefully. He was not afraid of the walking plants, for they moved slowly, but the Cocci-type hoppers whipped along with terrifying speed. He saw only one of the latter, walloping down the side of the Imbalancia, luckily moving away from him.

He looked toward the Black Ship. The gangway was down and he observed a man-shaped space suit explaining something with gestures to a pear-shaped space suit. Now was the time! He made a run for it, and arrived panting and speechless.

"Why, its Harp!" exclaimed the prince in a delighted voice. "You shouldn't run around without a suit. You'll get collected! Come in, quick!"

Harp ran up the gangplank and tumbled into the communal sitting room. Miss Squieze and Miss Constable were sitting at a table drinking tea, using both cups and saucers. The room was orderly and clean, there was a cloth upon the table and the pillows were plumped up. Now that he thought of it, the prince had looked a little strange. What was different? Only his head had poked out of the space suit. Yes, his hair was neatly trimmed and he was growing a moustache.

Harp tried to tell them about his adventures and misfortunes, but Miss Constable interrupted to inform him that he should now address Miss Squieze as Princess. "Of course I, as Lady-in-Waiting to her Highness and her closest friend, will continue to address her as Barbie," she added smugly.

"Oh, Harp," cried Princess Barbie, "Don't go back to Dr.

Fish. Stay with us. We thought you were going home to Earth with Tak, but since you didn't go, you can wait and travel back with us. We'll be leaving as soon as the Elf-star scare is over."

She began to list the improvements the royal pair planned to make on Earth as soon as they returned. Brute intended to start with the swimming pool, and she had thoughts about childhood vaccination and also some relaxation of the sumptuary laws, as she did not really see herself in red with her light complexion.

The others drifted into the room. Rodrigo spoke to Miss Constable in a voice that managed to be both firm and caressing at the same time. "How about fixing up a room for Harp three doors away from yours. And maybe you could show him how to work the shower, and he could use a haircut and a new coverall afterwards." He actually smiled. Harp noticed that both pirates were sporting short hair and that their beards were trimmed. Miss Constable scuttled away to obey orders.

Harp told them the sorry tale of his failed attempt to reach Earth, his confusion, the two Anebits, Tak's memory loss and the two Crystal Changers. Then he asked for a glass of clean unpolluted water if they had one. They were puzzled that he did not beg for alcohol, but said nothing.

However, after they had considered his story they had a good deal to say about the Elf-star, known as the Scourge of the Universe. "If you go back to Tak's water hole I think you will find two of him as well as two of everything else. You must have sailed right by the Elf-star on the way to Earth. Well, you were warned," grumbled Red Pat. "It doesn't do the cloning bit very often, but in that mood it's more dangerous than if it merely blew up a planet. That's really what they are afraid of here. If the Imbalancia got cloned it would probably mean the end of the Universe. Just imagine two identical supreme forces in competition," he mourned, and walked over to the communicator to notify the authorities.

"It wouldn't be such a bad thing if our ship got cloned. That would be one quick way of building up a fleet," chuckled Rodrigo, laughing at Pat's pessimism. Nobody wanted to mention anything more about cloning to Harp. They were all wondering the same thing: if the Crystal Changer and all its contents had been doubled, there should be a second identical Harp. Where was he? With that in mind the conversation remained evasively vague. They need not have bothered; even if they had come right out with it he would not have believed them. Only natural born identical twins are capable of knowing themselves to be two.

Harp drank his water and, because he was so warm and comfortable, sat back and began to snooze. He was rudely awakened by Miss Constable who led him down the hall and into his newly prepared cabin, where she sat in a straight chair waiting for him to finish showering, calling instructions from time to time. She had a new coverall for him when he came out and a sharp pair of scissors.

After she had perfected him as much as she could she left him with a glass of juice and some crackers. He lay back on the bed and sighed with contentment; it was a long time since he had lain flat on a bed. He rehearsed the places where he had slept in his short life. His mind dwelt on the hills of his childhood, the slag piles overgrown with stunted underbrush and twisted trees, their dwarfish limbs so flowery in summer and so desolate and naked in winter.

He thought about the sagging house on stilts which had been his home, of the little pool of fresh icy water that lay silently in the wet leaves near the top of the bench behind the house. There was no inlet to the pool; the water had risen by itself in the black-bottomed declivity. It was so clear that he could see the trash that had been thrown in during the years: mossy boards, tin cans, bottles, bones, coils of rusted wire. He wondered why he had never stopped to clear it out; it would have been easy.

The little spring had been all the mystery and adventure of his childhood. His bare feet had sunk through the matted ferns and felt the shocking cold. Another day he experimented and stirred the mud with his toes, making the bottom invisible. He laughed gleefully and stamped around it till he cut his foot on something sharp.

He saw all kinds of flying creatures and little forest animals that came to drink. He tasted it himself, drinking down the icy water in great gulps. He retired to its security when the shouts of his irascible father or the scoldings of his embittered mother drove him so far into himself that he needed to withdraw.

Overflowing, the frigid water had trickled down over the rocks until it reached the secret cave hiding the still. From there it filtered modestly out through pebbles and joined the narrow brook, which he had finally followed down to the big world, a main stream that traveled loudly, picking up all sorts of refuse, becoming progressively dirtier as it tumbled down the mountain to melt into the sluggish river below.

Longing for his home swept over Harp as he remembered not the blows he had received, not the hunger and boredom and general gay dirtiness salved with alcohol, but the smooth dark pool on the bench. There was the week of worrying when he had waited vainly for the return of his parents and instead received an unanswerable notice from the Welfare computer that they were dead, and that he also was recorded as dead. But when he had to leave home it was not the broken glass of the distillery he grieved for, or his mother's cooking; it was the pool.

He woke up and noticed that Miss Constable had left a glass of juice for him on the table. But he ignored it and made a bee-line for the bathroom. There he drank water from the tap, sometimes scooping it up and sometimes wedging his open mouth under the sputtering stream. He drank until his stomach hurt. It was not bad on the whole, but not equal to the woodland spring in his dream.

Miss Constable reappeared at the door. "Hurry-up, Harp. You have to help me fix supper. Rodrigo said I could have you as my assistant. Can you cook? No? Can you clean?"

"I'm sorry. I can boil water and stir mash. I can mop the floor. I can wash dishes. I like to see things clean." He notice that the corridor outside the door showed dirty footprints.

"Good," she said. "Now follow me into the kitchen. I know you'll be useful. You may call me Lou."

LEVIATHANS

The confused Tak had watched Harp climb out of the Crystal Changer, retrieve his rubber boat, climb in with the Anebit and start to row across the steaming pond that lay just within the door of the pressure chamber. The Radial was not sure what he should do next. The water looked inviting, a little like home, so he squirmed out of his space suit and tried it with the tip of a cautious tentacle.

It felt wonderful and so with a kind of reckless happiness he slipped in, rolled over a few times to restore his nerves, and set out on a swim of exploration. He had not long to search, for almost at once his body collided with that of his double.

"Forgive me, Master," he said in the gasps and gurgles with which Radials communicate, "I did not mean to bump you; I was not expecting another occupant. You live here also, I presume? I am Tak, the navigator of the Imbalancia. I have recently been ill and am not yet quite recovered."

Horror froze Tak Major (as we must now designate him to differentiate him from the newer Tak minor, because he had indeed lost some of his attributes and was less now than he had been before.)

Tak Major was only stunned for a moment, but Radials do not know fear and he grappled with the stranger who grappled with him in return. Their tentacles became interwoven as they tensed in a terrible underwater struggle. They glared into each other's eyes, one at a time, because since Radials have eyes on opposite sides of their heads they can not focus properly on nearby objects. But they knew each other at once. Each attempted to crush his opponent in long undulating coils. The huge thrashing ball they made rolled over and over in the hissing water. Occasionally a single tentacle extricated itself from the mass and dove in for a stronger hold. The water bubbled with their gurgling cries of rage.

The battle should have been equal but who better than Tak Major knew their joint weaknesses? Certainly not Tak minor, who had the same weaknesses but had forgotten them along with nearly everything else. Grief and fasting had further enfeebled him.

Tak Major craftily seized with his sharp beak a very small shriveled tentacle that his opponent carried, as did he himself, curled up and tucked away in a safe place. It was a sore one which had been carried rolled up like that for Radial generations, ever since it had developed a tendency to manufacture lactic acid at its slightest movement. The brain connected to it functioned erratically under acid stimulus, so both the brain and limb had been deactivated temporarily in the expectation of amputation at a much later date after Tak Major had steeled himself for a visit to the orthoextractor.

When Tak Major's beak bit into the limb and when its corresponding brain awoke, the pain caused Tak minor to scream for mercy and confess himself beaten. "I'll do anything you say," he moaned. "Oh, how did this happen to me!"

Tak Major loosened his hold upon his opponent's body and transferred his grip upon the tortured tentacle from his beak to one of his arms in order to be able to speak.

"For one thing, because you are me and not just you," said Tak Major aggressively, and demanded an explanation while feeling about all over his motionless opponent's body for anything concealed in his pockets. There were a number of useful articles, duplicates of his own, and these he transferred to his own storage pouches.

The explanation provided by Tak minor was incomplete, of course, for he was already beginning to forget his return trip to the Imbalancia and he garbled the tale badly. He was unable to account for Harp properly, though he remembered him slightly and even recalled that they had alighted at the Imbalancia simultaneously. Tak Major lifted one eye above the surface on the roiled water and observed Harp hauling his boat onto the ledge.

He released his captive-self and swam over to the pressure chamber, and unobserved by Harp, who was busy eating, lifted himself out of the water and crawled in. He discovered the duplicate Crystal Changer and immediately guessed what had happened. They had met the Elf-Star in one of its blacker moods and now he, Tak, the unique, would have to contend with a double, an extra inexcusable Crystal Changer and possibly (his thoughts brightened) another Anebit.

He looked hopefully toward his refrigerator and saw Harp preparing to go to sleep on the inflated raft. And near him lay his own plastic wrapped Anebit where he had left it, and beside it was its twin. He shuddered with delight.

Because the new Tak had no recollection of having left Harp on Earth, the duplication must have occurred before that point. Which meant that the original Harp was on Earth where he could cause them no trouble; the main points to contend with were his double and extra Crystal Changer.

But he had to report the run-in with the Elf-star. It must be remembered that the whereabouts of the Elf-star were known only by the events surrounding its appearance, which were defined as uniformly enforceable and never following any known physical laws. He located the approximate coordinates of the fateful meeting by drawing a mental line between the Imbalancia and Earth and approximating the time distance between Earth and the unlikely vomiting fit that he suspected had something to do with it. Activating his speaking tube, he alerted the authorities.

This executive duty accomplished, and with the knowledge that the Imbalancia would be held motionless and silent for some time longer to evade the marauding Elf-star, and that the surface of the planet would be held inviolate long enough for him to travel on it unseen and dispose of the unwanted Crystal Changer, he faced the moral problem of the ownership of the second Anebit.

He felt that he had the right to both of them. At the same time he knew that Tak minor, as soon as he had his wits about him, would demand his half. Therefore it might be necessary to paralyze or dispose of his rival, whom he now saw had sunk thoroughly cowed into a corner of the pool and was crying to himself.

The vanquished Tak minor lifted his grief-stricken head out of the water at his alter-ego's approach. The throbbing had left his wounded limb but he was unhappy even without that painful stimulus.

"What's the matter?" asked Tak Major, knowing from the way he felt himself what was the matter.

"Matter? Matter? Here I am perfectly helpless, not remembering my identity, with you biting me and not knowing what to do to prevent another similar occurrence, and not even knowing your intentions toward me. Oh, dear me." He wept again.

"We are one and the same," said Tak Major severely. "Take my word for it that I am no more capable of destroying you than I am of destroying myself. Don't worry about that. The only question is how shall we reunite and achieve some semblance of respectability again. We cannot continue this dual existence for long; it will attract attention and will be extremely uncomfortable. I shall have to repress you in some way until you cease to have an independent existence."

"Master, do not repress me! I want to live." wailed the minor Tak.

"You are not going to die. Not literally. I considered devouring you but you are too large, and besides I am not sure that it would achieve the desired result. Perhaps if you were speechless and remained out of sight under water..."

"But what would I do there, or even think about? I want some happiness and space to swim in, too."

"Do? Do? Who cares what you do. I only wish to get rid of you. Look after yourself, after all, I have to. Nobody looks after me!"

"Master, let me bring you some water-weed cake. I had not

realized you were hungry," said Tak minor eagerly. "I started to make some while I was under water weeping and waiting for you. It will be as light as a feather, a recipe that I just invented, flavored with the divine Lauchet."

A truce was declared while Tak Major ate the cake, which had been sogging and blooming in the steam all the while they talked. It was true, the new Tak had been constructing it idly with some of his tentacles while he was grieving with the rest of him, for the minds and limbs of the Radials are restless and cannot bear inactivity.

The cake was delicious; Tak Major ate and enjoyed it. He had never thought that he would enjoy eating, but with its superior flavor and the opportunity to chat while chewing, a luxury he had not enjoyed since leaving Vpor so long ago, he finished it quickly and even toyed with the idea of wanting more. He also felt more optimistic.

"Very well," he said, "You may do the cooking. You can invent any new dishes you wish, you may come up from under water at the hours I select, you may upon invitation think in tandem with me on difficult problems. At times you may chat in your dataless way for I enjoy the sound of it. And it may be, but mind you I am promising nothing, that I shall some day allow you to help me navigate the Imbalancia. But remember, it will not be a regular treat as I am quite satisfied with the assistance of my Anebit."

"Yes, Gracious Master," was Tak minor's meek reply.

Tak Major raised his head to see what Harp was doing. He noticed immediately that the two Anebits were gone and that Harp was gone, too. He swam over to the area just below the ledge to make sure that none of them had fallen into the water. There was no sign of them; no hot cross Anebits, no parboiled Harp.

He saw that both the door to the pressure chamber and the door leading to the outside were open. Harp must have stolen the Anebits and run away with them. He swam to the pressure chamber and leaned out the door leading to the planet surface. No sign of Harp. But he did notice some human-sized foot prints pointing in the direction of the Black Ship. He could see that Harp had gained sanctuary, so the deprived and infuriated Radial could only curl and uncurl his tentacles and snap his beak in unproductive rage.

A pair of peculiar fat birds flew by his face, just missing one of his eyes. He knew them at once. "Come back," he howled, but they flirted their stubby little tails and flew on.

Tak Major returned frustrated to his pool, having finally remembered the necessity of hiding one of the Crystal Changers. He took one of Harp's pails and filled it with water weed. Next he opened the cover of a tentacle sized opening high on a wall and took out a tightly capped bottle. He poured the contents into the pail where they started to fizz. He opened another hole and sent a prying tentacle inside. Out came a bottle of something else. It was a powder and it caused an even greater reaction when he added it to the concoction he was mixing.

"May I ask what you are doing, Master?"

"This powerful chemical compound which I have just invented, utilizing some of my neighbors' stores, will be used to mar the shining surface of one of the two Crystal Changers. When we are through it will be so roughened that no one will be able to distinguish it from an old wart on the Imbalancia. Once it is disguised in this manner I can keep it for myself in case I want to travel in a hurry. It can also be used as another room in the event that I get tired of your company."

"You are going to trust me to help you?"

"Yes, you can do the painting while I return the other Changer to its proper place under the Imbalancia. I don't like to get my own tentacles dirty, and besides the mixture might burn. No one will notice us working as they are all indoors hiding under their beds for fear of the Elf-star."

They lumbered out, Tak Major carrying the pail. Tak minor, who was not entirely stupid, brought the strip of discarded plastic which had once enveloped the Anebit, to protect his painting arm.

The missing chute was under the floor of the pressure

chamber. Tak Major flipped it into place, then prodded his double onto it and slid down afterwards, gingerly holding the paint pail.

The climb up the side of the Imbalancia was not too difficult, as the minor Tak had an arm span of nearly fifteen feet as well as groups of strategically-placed suction cups. He received plenty of prodding from behind. When he was settled on top of the Crystal Changer, Tak Major handed up the pail and then left to return the duplicate vehicle to its own proper place, leaving his subordinate to get down afterwards as best he could.

Tak minor painted over the surface with a swathed tentacle; every stroke satisfactorily roughened and blistered the mirror finish. He was enjoying himself and worked busily until there was only the unpainted circle left beneath his body. Then, of course, he wished to rest somewhere else so he could finish painting the shining circle on top.

Not only was there nowhere else to sit except on the summit of the changer, but he did not see any way to get himself down except by a sliding free fall and resultant marring of his own hide on the corrosive paint.

He sat and thought. He could not find any solution though he put all of his heretofore unused brains to work, separately and then in sequence. There was one good result. It was the first time in his young cloned life that his multiple brains had been exercised and he found that they worked very well indeed. For one thing, he realized how Tak Major had tricked him into this situation, indeed, he now understood his elder brother thoroughly, and upon observing his smirking approach to rescue him by handing up the end of the chute so he could slide down inside, resolved to keep secret his newly obtained omniscience.

"Oh Master, I never could have got down by myself. Thank you, Thank you!" he gushed hypocritically, planning an appropriate revenge.

They went back inside where Tak Major relayed an order on his translator for flax seeds to be set out for the Anebits in case they returned.

He was right, for they did return to crunch the seeds as

long as the Imbalancia remained on the planet. No one knew where they made their nest or whether they stayed behind or not when the ship later departed. They had spilled a number of seeds on the ground which grew up into pretty blue flowers. Over the years they spread until the entire surface of the planet was covered with them, and navigators who spotted it in their scopes named it the Blue Planet.

It goes without saying that the Aubudon Society was incensed at this ecological carelessness, and added one more demerit to Tak Major's portfolio of sins. But there was nothing they could do to punish him, for they had only one navigator. They also knew about the Crystal Changer but said nothing; it was a waste of time to try to keep secrets on the Imbalancia, for microscopic-sized delegates sometimes made a career out of espionage.

The two Taks left their doors open so the Anebits could fly in if they wished and the top of the Crystal changer was left unpainted so the light reflected from it might serve as a beacon for the flying computers. But they never returned to their former owners.

The two Radials settled down to play their mental games, and they were so successful that Tak Major found the Anebits unnecessary for the navigation of the ship now that the two of them could think so well both in sequence and in opposition. It was no time at all before Tak Major led his counterpart through a series of manholes, tunnels and self-opening doors into the very bowels of the Imbalancia, to behold the essential gravo-drive. They spent many happy hours there planning improvements to the system and giving orders to a multitude of sub-microscopic assistants who cared for the massive machinery, penetrating all of its parts with their willing little bodies.

There was hope among the leaders of the Society that the new Tak could someday learn to be the navigator and Tak Major could be sent home to Vpor in disgrace. But perhaps Tak Major anticipated their intentions, for he failed to teach his twin some of the more vital processes.

The two of them were so busy that they forgot to be angry at Harp. You must remember that their memories were not very good. It was harder for them to forget the Anebits, but they managed it, sometimes even forgetting to re-fill their flax seed container.

Harp had forgotten about the Radials fairly well also, for all the residents of the Black Ship were happily absorbed in making plans for their futures. Princess Barbie had been disappointed to discover that her husband was little more than a nominal ruler, unable to command anything beyond the area around the palace. But he was enormously rich and money is a kind of power, too. If he couldn't order it he could buy it, which was more civilized and polite anyway.

Harp thought it might be nice to be rich and wondered how he could accomplish such a goal. Pat was now the gloomy one of the two pirates and grumbled about the lack of anything to drink, while Rodrigo bore a constant furtive grin on his face. Pat suggested that Harp return to Tak's pond and talk him into distilling some more water-weed gin.

"No," said Harp. "Not possible. The big guy's gone crazy." He repeated the story of his wild ride with Tak minor at the controls of the Crystal changer, so rather than hear it again, Pat had to resign himself to yet another dry evening.

"Jesus, it would really have been something to see if he had been driving the Imbalancia in that condition," hooted Rodrigo in his new jollity.

"Good thing he doesn't remember much about the past; if he did he might want to get drunk again," said Harp virtuously, having forgotten his own previous predilections. "I don't believe he ever tasted booze before he distilled it. I guess it's a good thing he doesn't remember how. Let's not tell him. It's pretty bad stuff and it leads to most of the problems in the Universe." They stared at him in disbelief.

"I'd really like to get back to Earth soon. I used to live in a beautiful spot: woods, pure water, a simple unpolluted environment, a life close to Nature. Trouble is, without money I can't go back there to stay."

"We're stuck here all right," Pat moaned.

"Don't be so sour," said his companion. "Buck up! Show the kid around the ship. We've plenty of visitors."

"And diamonds, rubies and emeralds," jeered Pat.

"I meant to ask," said Harp. "Are those really diamonds and rubies and emeralds all over the ground outside?"

"Nah," said Pat. "Only a few rubies, sapphires, malachite in plenty, and quartz but not diamonds. They're not worth the transport. Besides, how would we smuggle them into the cities to sell? I can just see us landing secretly on a desert island and swimming to market with water-wings and our mouths full of gems. The only thing we can sell on Earth is our gold, which we earn very slowly fair and square. Bah! We're stranded here in Space until we die, and that's all there is to it!"

"Harp!" yelled Miss Constable from the kitchen, "come and help me serve dinner!" She hurried in with a pile of plates and Harp ran into the kitchen and emerged with a steaming bowl. Miss Constable had changed out of her white nurse's coverall and was now clothed clingingly in a large piece of turquoise shot silk held in place just below her breasts by a black cumberbund. Several gold chains encircled her neck, one was entwined in her hair and a number of rings with flashing stones adorned her fingers. She wore eye shadow and looked altogether different; everyone exclaimed over her appearance except the glum-faced Pat.

They ate eagerly. Lou was good cook and Harp an enthusiastic assistant. The kitchen was no longer the repository of bachelor clutter and Harp was beginning to examine the pipes of the water system, looking for signs of pollution.

"For God's sake, Harp, don't discuss sewage while we're eating," scolded the princess.

"But it's very important. The filters are in terrible condition, bacteria are growing everywhere and the hydroponics are a disaster. Our very existence is in danger once our internal lithosphere is out of balance! I've been going over the whole thing and am finding...."

"Shut up!" yelled the prince in defense of his mate, who started to whimper. They all finished eating very crossly and the royal pair retired to go to their quarters. Harp was sent out to do the dishes, Rodrigo took Lou to his room to show her something, and Pat remained alone brooding. After a while he went out to help Harp.

"I'd try to avoid irritating the bridegroom if I were you. While you're part of the ship's crew you'll be O.K., but you're a freshly hatched chicken without enough brains to peck seeds off the ground. If you can keep the prince happy you'll do fine. Just try to agree with him all the time and run little errands for his wife. And stick close.

"Speaking of pecking seeds off the ground, there's nothing to prevent you from tucking a small handful of rubies and sapphires into your pockets, only one to a pocket, and well rubbed in bread crumbs. No emeralds, though. They can be picked up by the scanner. I'll tell you where to sell them and that should give you enough to build your cabin. But remember, only the prince can get you permission to build on preserved land. Now that he's twenty-one they're making him the Aubudon Society's official representative on Earth and he will make all decisions in their name, with half a dozen advisors leaning over his shoulder, of course. I've been listening in on the translator. Remember, the watch word is 'Kid Gloves'."

He led Harp into the hidden parts of the ship and Harp, with his new environmental obsession, studied everything, searching out flaws and giving interminable advice until Pat brought him forcibly back to the common sitting room. The others had returned; Brute was in an especially expansive mood, and he partly listened while Harp went on about his examination of the pipes.

The prince, who had heard just a little of the diatribe, said, "I may be able to use you at the palace. There we often have rust in the tap water and I have some rather complex plans for the swimming pool. As you know, all the water in Bostown is pumped from the sea, filtered and desalinated. It's not very nice. Perhaps you can do something about that. I've been wondering what to do with you when we return. I can't just buy you a ticket on the tourist tube;

you're so incompetent that you wouldn't be able to survive as a normal citizen. Therefore I'll have to appoint you to a Civil Service post to keep you alive. Well, something is sure to turn up when we get back to the palace."

"You're such a kind Brute," whispered the princess.

"I guess I'd better thank you, Prince," said Harp, though secretly he was dismayed at the thought of drinking desalinated water and suspected that he would have to read many hard books in order to hold a job as official palace plumber. "I'll make myself as useful as possible."

"I'll find plenty of work for you, for I intend to make great changes at the palace when I return. The first to go will be Dr. Dapper, who used to make my life a living Hell. Then I'll throw out his wife and set my sisters free. I'll invite all sorts of interesting people to the palace that they wouldn't approve of. I may even leave in disguise and travel through the tube to the outside world to see what is going on. Harp will go with me, of course, as my guide."

Everyone murmured their approval.

"I'm going to have to be in charge of the environment, so I'd better look at it. They've just told me about my new responsibilities on the communicator; I'm to be the Society's agent on Earth and am to meet with the Security Council for instructions this evening. They are sending me and Barbie down in the Crystal Changer in three days along with a team of teachers and advisors. You'll love it, Barbie."

Harp thought that if he was going to be the prince's guide he would guide him to the secret spring for a good drink of clean water. That is, if he could find it. They would have to follow the big river to its source, but there were so many sources. He felt confused; he had received so much good advice and learned so many facts that he was ready for a nap.

"Come on, Harp. I have to say good-bye to my old friends and I need you to show me the way to Tak's place. The Security Council people told me that I must try to maintain all the contacts I made here. They may come in handy one day."

As they started climbing into the space suits, of which the Black Ship had a good supply in all sizes, the mentally overloaded

Harp felt very sorry for himself, resigned as he was to a future of hard thinking. Suddenly he had a bright idea: if he followed the prince, doing what he was told with a big smile on his face, perhaps he would not have to think at all.

STRANGE FRUIT

They dressed in their helmetless space suits and went to visit the two Taks first. Harp knew that there were two Radials because he had been told so, but he found it difficult to accept. He led the prince across the jeweled ground to the Taks' chute, which still dangled from the doorway. They climbed up and made their clumsy way into the pressure chamber.

Harp noticed that there was now only one Crystal Changer; its door was open and when he looked in he was surprised to find it nearly dark inside. He hoped that the Radials had departed in the other Crystal Changer, but no such luck. He could see the water inside their pond bubbling, and the sight of two large heads emerging from the steam and staring at them with bulging eyes made him feel very uneasy, as he expected them to demand the whereabouts of the Anebits. He tried to hide behind his companion but the Radials hardly noticed him and addressed only the authoritive form of the prince.

"Greetings, Earth man," said one. And the other said "Congratulations on your elevation, Your Highness." The prince bowed.

Harp noticed a disturbance in the water at some distance from the aliens. It looked like a tangled mat of tentacles, about the right size to fit in a pail if it had been a mop. He feared that one of their limbs had fallen off, entangled itself, and was going through a death struggle. He wondered if he should mention it but the bundle suddenly jumped a foot in the air and plunged back into the water for a dive, and he saw that it was a small replica of the Radials themselves, though with proportionately shorter limbs.

"Look," he shouted. "Look at that!" But the others were still exchanging formalities and paid no attention to him. The little tentacled bundle was now advancing on a Radial. It scurried through the mass of writhing limbs and clambered fearlessly onto one of the large heads, where it started to work pecking the Radial at great speed with its tiny bill.

Tak Major ignored it and continued speaking but his speech was interrupted with cries of pain and futile attempts to wipe off the interloper with his thrashing tentacles.

The little creature became bored with its woodpecker game and slid off to flounder through the entwined limbs of the other Tak. This time it approached the Radial's open mouth, stretched it wider with its own small limbs, stuck its beak inside and administered some terrible punishment, so much so that poor Tak minor sank into the water, crying out and thrashing in vain to dislodge the diminutive attacker.

Even the prince, engaged in diplomatic exchanges, could not help exclaiming at this but the Radials seemed to take the disturbance for granted. Their heads were both out of the water now and the smaller version of themselves was cavorting and doing fancy dives at a distance.

"What is that?" demanded the prince.

"What, where?" was the evasive response.

"That ferocious little thing."

"Oh, that. That's a jelly pup; they are common enough on Vpor. We don't pay much attention to it," said one of the Radials. "It just appeared this morning."

"We have no idea where it came from," said the other.

Harp thought it was a young Radial, and said so.

"Perhaps," was the dual reply. They both looked fondly at the jelly pup and one of them chased it with a tentacle until it was caught, then wrapped it up and gave it a good shaking and stared morosely into one of its eyes. It started to wiggle and gurgle.

Harp was reminded of Tak's behavior toward his Anebit.

Now the Radials' attention was entirely absorbed by the jelly pup and they had not yet mentioned the Anebits' disappearance and his own culpability. He felt brave enough to address them and to say thank-you for caring for him and saving his life. He did not know which of them to thank, so he spoke to both of them.

But they were so busy that they barely noticed him, and the prince drew him away from the steamy chamber. They slid down to the ground and walked the short distance to the door of the delegates' cell.

The chute was lowered and neither of the doors was properly locked, though as far as they knew the delegates still considered the outside climate to be lethal. When they entered the cubicle they received no more than a disinterested greeting from Wiener, who was puttering around with some wires and solder.

"Oh, there you are," he muttered. "We were wondering what had happened to you. You both look O.K."

They could hear voices raised in consternation through the port leading into the Fastar. The door had been fastened open with a bent wire and the flight of steps leading up to it was more sturdily built than usual.

"What are they yelling about?" asked Harp as he climbed out of his space suit. The prince unsuited also.

"Where did you get the new clothes, Harp? And what happened to your helmets?"

"Oh, that," said the prince, lying smoothly. "We got them from a local outfitter. Our space suits are new, too. They're the kind that don't need helmets."

Wiener examined Harp's suit, squeezing the wiring through the thick fabric. He wrinkled his forehead as he played with the controls, getting warm air and then cool air. He started to turn the suit inside out.

"What's all the fuss about in the Fastar?" repeated Harp.

"Oh, that." Wiener reluctantly turned his attention away from the suit. "They're having trouble with the babies. An unexplained phenomenon. They've merged. Irma put them in the same crib to get acquainted and turned her back. When she looked around they had merged. A complete mix. Two heads, and then four legs attached at random, one growing out of the girl's arm, another sticking out of the boy's arm, everything else wrong, too, fingers and toes all over the place. The effect is pretty ugly. And the damn brats think its funny; they laugh all the time and Irma's been screaming for the last couple of days."

"Good God, what are you going to do about it?"

"We've tried to figure out how to get them apart, but pulling doesn't help and we can't even locate the joins; there are no seams at all. But apparently they can change at will, for when they're not watched they swap parts so fast you can't see them. They're testing the theory that the kids will take it into their heads to separate some time or another and then they can be grabbed and kept apart. We're taking turns watching them in order to be ready when the time comes. I just came off duty. It's a hell of a job and a disgusting sight."

"Maybe we'd better stay out of there," Harp said cautiously.

"Maybe you'd better if you don't want to take a turn watching," agreed Wiener, continuing his interrupted examination of the space suit.

"Got anything to eat?" asked Harp.

"Sure," said Wiener, preoccupied. "There's some Hydro paste in that can. Just add hot water from the kettle. Spoons are on the shelf."

The prince refused politely, as Harp prepared and ate some of the mush. He was not very hungry but had been curious to see if he would be accepted in his new role of fellow human, or if the others would try to force his old intravenous tube back on him, or alcohol in a bottle, or sugar in some form, thus re-establishing him as an experimental subject. But now he was not afraid of them, as he had the prince for protection. He had been prepared to demand recognition as a guest at dinner and was delighted that the first move had gone off so well. A new feeling of importance flowed through him; it gave him far greater strength than mere food could.

The strength ebbed momentarily when Dr. Fish's cameo face appeared in the doorway. Whatever her intentions had been at that moment, she forgot them at the sight of the visitors.

She gave a polite nod to the prince and then spoke severely to Harp. "Where did you come from? Well, never mind. It doesn't matter in the least because I have no time for you. I will continue to give you your feedings, on demand, for as long as you need them, but you can't expect me to take an interest in your case. I am far too busy. Besides, your value is doubtful; the experiment was discontinued prematurely. I'm sorry, but that's how it is." She shied away from the opening, and they could hear her clear high voice rising above the others' as she plunged once more into the problem of the merged babies.

Word got around quickly that Harp and the prince had returned, for both Irma and Al came to the port to see them. Al lowered himself through the opening and asked Harp amiably about his adventures.

Harp exaggerated his story a little and did not say much about the Black Ship and his two new friends, since they had been instrumental in the abduction of the nurses. Instead he played up the story of the water-weed gin and the imbibings of the naive Tak as well as the confused Radial's dependence upon Harp's help and guidance. He boasted of the way he had directed the Crystal Changer back to the Imbalancia and informed them that he was planning to return to Earth as an assistant and guide to the prince.

His audience was amazed but as the prince denied nothing, only rolled up his eyes a little, they did not protest.

Al was most struck, not by the improbable adventures, but by Harp's failure to make any mention of a craving for alcohol. This puzzled him considerably.

"Has your urge to drink diminished appreciably?" he asked with as much delicacy as his curiosity would allow.

"Gave it up," said Harp. "I knew it wasn't healthy, so I decided to quit."

"Just like that?"

"Just like that. I always do what I make up my mind to

do."

"But wasn't it awfully difficult? I mean physically, that is."

"No, and I feel like a new man. Should have tried it years ago."

"But it's physically addicting," Al insisted.

"Can't you talk about something else?" asked Harp, and sidled over to the port where he climbed up on the cans and peered in. He drew back with an audible gasp.

"Horrible," he advised the prince. "It's a monstrosity: it makes you sick just to look at it. It's got two rear ends and it's just messed out of one of them. I can't bear to look at it." He backed away from the port in disgust.

"Don't they do mercy killing for that sort of thing?" he asked after a moment's thought.

"Listen, they're my kids," said Al, who had crumpled into a corner.

"Or mine," reminded Wiener.

The head of the Rda appeared through the open port; he seemed to be enjoying himself. "So very amusing and instructive for those who will derive a lesson from it," he pronounced with his lips pursed in a satisfied smirk. "It just goes to show that the younger generation can never be totally controlled or shaped, but must be allowed to develop according to their inborn tendencies. Even my mild reproofs were ignored when I asked the little darlings to re-form properly. So strong-willed, just like their mother and, of course, their father." The remainder of his body poured through the porthole and lay in a shining silvery coil on the floor while his head drooped at conversational height, hooked onto a convenient staple by one of his flexible antennae.

Irma's face, red with fury, poked through the door. "You Devil! It's all your fault; you taught them that trick. I know you did. Well, you can just leave. And you can take the damn brats with you. I never want to see you or them again!"

"Are you sure?" The Rda turned his head as he hung easily from the coiled antenna so he could look directly at Irma. "Are you sure you really mean it? Reflect, be careful, and do not be over-hasty."

"I mean it all right. I never want to see your ugly face or their ugly backsides again!"

"Thank you," said the Rda, politely and sincerely. "I have only been waiting for your permission." He disappeared from the staple as he spoke.

"Coming in here nosing around," said Al belligerently, "claiming to be their father!" But Irma had disappeared too; she had gone back in to look at the children. All was apparently quiet in the Fastar; the children no longer cried or babbled.

Dr. Fish appeared at the porthole. Her face was white. "I think you had better step in here," she whispered. "The children have vanished."

Vanished they had and return they did not. While Al and Wiener and Dr. Fish were all commanding one another to call the authorities, Harp and the prince managed to coax the shocked mother into Harp's space suit. When she complained about the lack of a helmet, they pulled a plastic bag with air holes poked into it over her head, which seemed to satisfy her in her dazed condition. Then Harp and the prince each held a sleeve of her suit for symbolic protection from the roving Cocci Hoppers, and the three of them slipped and stumbled over the gravel to the gangplank of the Black Ship, pulled Irma up the ramp and handed her over to the two nurses, who put her to bed.

A curious thing happened as a result of all the excitement and shouting. Someone had left the door of the monkey's cage open, perhaps looking for the co-joined babies inside, and the clever little primate, who had been watching and waiting for such an opportunity, stole over to the pressure chamber, turned the handle, scrambled through the chute and ran free.

Of course this freedom did not last long as the monkey was seized almost at once by a Cocci Hopper and borne in triumph to the local representatives of the Society for the Collection of endangered Species. They kept it there for some time until Tak Major, who regularly traveled through nearly all parts of the Imbalancia, recognized its species and insisted on returning it to its native jungle, an expensive and lengthy operation. The monkey was quite surprised, for it had never known anything but a laboratory cage.

EPILOGUE

Al and Rodrigo deposited Harp in a secluded area with his pockets full of gold dust and rubies, plus a few modern coins to buy himself a ticket to the National Cemetery where he was to meet his old friends. Once there he mingled with the worshipers and made his way cautiously to the palace, keeping his eye peeled for any Horsemen in the neighborhood. His manner was so furtive that some of them looked at him a bit askance.

But he reached the palace door successfully, and after showing a pass with which the prince had provided him, was invited in and given a comfortable bedroom with a shower bath, a TV and a clock. There was also a bookcase full of easy books, selected for him by Princess Barbie, who was already an authority figure of no mean proportions.

Harp was not entirely at ease living with the royal family; his dream of following the prince around and taking orders and giving advice went unfulfilled. Instead he was driven into the society of the princesses. Now that his hair had grown out and the last traces of his acne had faded, he was a fairly good looking fellow. He was also somewhat older, as evinced by the hairs on his chin, which had grown from boyish fuzz into a proper beard. They were all older. What had seemed to be only a few days on the far off planet was considerably longer, for they had failed to take into consideration its very slow rotation. The princesses hung about him shamelessly, hugging him and asking questions, until Princess Barbie hired a retired female professor of astronomy to play the double role of chaperon and governess. While Barbie wished to guard the virginity of her sisters-in-law, the prince intended to send them to the Imbalancia in order to enlarge their experience; but only after they had learned a bit more about their duty toward the environment.

All the princesses wanted was to have Harp escort them to the Horsemen's stable where they were taking riding lessons on the retired horses, which were allowed to hang around until they died of old age. They were safe animals and very well trained. Watched by the lady professor the girls rode round and round under the shouted tutelage of a good humored bow-legged man named Captain Bothwell. The three princesses adored horses above all things, and seeing that Harp was deeply impressed by the great shining brutes, insisted that he ride also.

At first he was terrified, but realizing that his elderly mount held no grudge against him, indeed, was incapable of any such emotion, he found himself suddenly so tall that he felt like a God, and joined the princesses joyfully in the ring and practiced starting and stopping while the girls went bravely over tiny jumps. Afterwards he helped them rub down their steeds and muck out the stalls while Captain Bothwell shouted orders at them and the amused stablemen looked on, chewing bits of hay. He secretly gave his horse his greatest treasure, the little plastic wrapped packet of sugar which he still carried next to his heart for an emergency. The horse gazed at him in affectionate gratitude.

The prince had a badge made for Harp upon which was stamped "Captain of the Royal Horse". He wore it with pride on his blue and silver uniform. When he walked in the cemetery and encountered groups of Horsemen they saluted him with perfect seriousness. He was very happy and knew that he would be secure for the rest of his life, with a salary and a pension to follow. Which was just as well, for his gold dust and rubies had been lost in the wash.

Barbie remembered his little spring in the woods, and after locating it on a map ordered a small lodge to be built there on the site of the McCuddy shack, where the royal couple could vacation in privacy. Harp was given a key and visited frequently at first, but less often as time went by. He always brought back some sweet mountain water in a canteen, which he thoughtfully shared with the others.

Instead of listening only to the vagaries of Harp, the prince pulled his political strings at the Aubudon Society and had Al and Wiener recalled and replaced with new delegates. He took Dr. Al Kapital into his household to advise him on managing his small principality, for the prince needed some relief from the advice of the six strange creatures that had come down from the Imbalancia with him and which now lived in specially adapted rooms at the palace.

Dr. Wiener von Brane was sent to the University with recommendations for a Chair. The prince was in the habit of donating large sums to the University and dabbling in its affairs; they were currently engaged in a project to re-write all the history books according to his and Barbie's instructions. With Wiener went the lovely Eustacia and her cat. Her name was now an object of ridicule in the research branch of the medical profession due to her well publicized intergalactic goof-up. After publishing a few badly received articles on disguised poisons she drifted into what was for her the correct niche, the Drama Department, where she starred in all the faculty plays and joyfully earned the undying hatred of the other faculty wives. Wiener had sneaked a few specimens of plant life back from the planet where they had lately stayed, and made a good thing of them.

The Black Ship remained on Earth only long enough to drop Harp off and to stock up for the next celestial voyage. They sold their gold and placed an order for another ship, as well as for new furnishings for the old one. After their next voyage Red Pat would be the captain of one and Rodrigo captain of the other.

The pirates had made life so pleasant for Lou and Irma that they decided not to disembark except to go shopping. Their worried husbands followed them at a little distance without being observed, to make sure no one lured them away, but there was nothing to fear. Both pirates now smiled most of the time.

After a few months the bemused Irma gave birth to another baby which quickly became fat and pink, and sucked its thumb and hardly ever cried. Whatever she and Lou asked for was imported regardless of expense or difficulty. Seconded by Lou, who could be quite formidable in her role of Miss Constable, Irma would never allow any of their celestial customers to enter their living quarters for fear of infection, and when the two pirates climbed up the gangway after business excursions they had to stand in a tub of disinfectant one minute before they were allowed over the threshold.

What became later of the prince and his friends is still unknown. But with their brides, Rodrigo and Pat established the dynasty of the Black Ship Trading Company that eventually replaced the Aubudon Society as the controlling force in the Universe, exploring galaxies and expanding intergalactic commerce under the watchful eye of the all-knowing and all-powerful Elf-star.

ABOUT THE AUTHOR

Ann Kucera is a native of Canada and thinks of her life as a series of fresh starts. Her wide range of experiences has made her the writer she is today. The author is a member of MENSA as well as an active participant in the ISPE.

Ms. Kucera is a published writer in various genres including poetry and essays on science and philosophy. She is currently working on a short story collection and compiling research focused on gifted children. The author is married with three children, and resides in the beautiful but chilly state of Maine.